It Happened In Illinois

Remarkable Events That Shaped History

Richard Moreno

Guilford, Connecticut

Copyright © 2011 by Morris Book Publishing, LLC

Project editor: Meredith Dias
Layout: Joanna Beyer
Map: Daniel Lloyd © Morris Book Publishing, LLC

Library of Congress Cataloging-in-Publication Data is available on file.

ISBN 978-0-7627-6128-9

Printed in the United States of America

10 9 8 7 6 5 4 3 2 1

CONTENTS

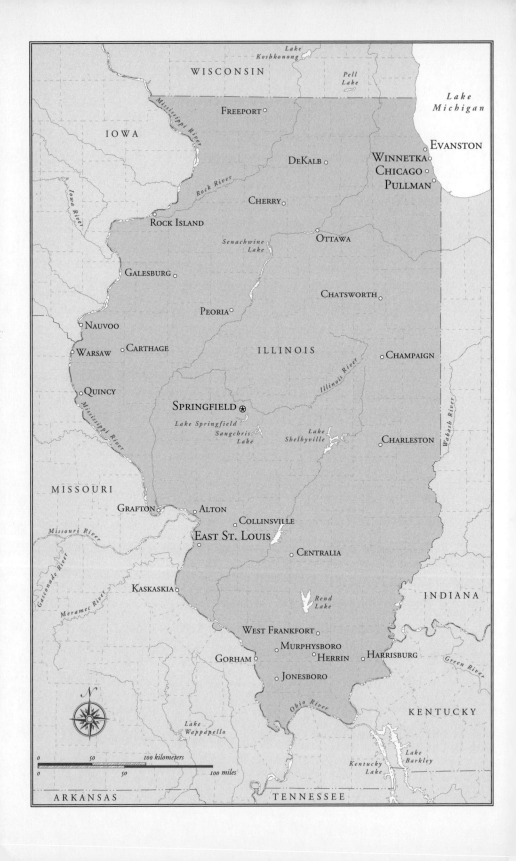

ACKNOWLEDGMENTS

I am grateful to a handful of people and institutions for generously providing assistance during the preparation of this book. In particular, I would like to thank the staff members of the Western Illinois University Malpass Library for their help in locating and obtaining many of the research books and articles used to write this work. I would also like to thank my past and present Globe Pequot Press editors, including Allen Jones, Erin Turner, and Meredith Rufino, for giving me an incentive to explore and learn about a whole new state. Additionally, I'd like to thank my wife, Pam, and my daughter, Julia, and my son, Hank, for patiently listening when I read them various passages and portions of the manuscript and for offering valuable insights and suggestions throughout the writing and editing process. Lastly, I dedicate this book to my parents, Richard and Maureen Moreno, who have always been there for me.

INTRODUCTION

I first visited Illinois in the late 1980s when I went to Chicago on a business trip. I had lived nearly my entire life in the West, with the exception of a year in New York City, so the place fascinated me. I recall that Richard M. Daley, who ended up being the city's mayor for several decades, was then running for that office for the first time, and I was intrigued by how everyone in the city seemed so interested in the election—something I'd not experienced in California or Nevada. Politics was an active topic of conversation, just like the Cubs were, and everyone had an opinion (like they always do about the Cubs). I wasn't in town long, but I managed to stop at the Billy Goat Tavern for a "cheezborger" and a beer (an Old Style), ate a Chicago-style hot dog, and wandered through some of the stores on the Magnificent Mile (North Michigan Avenue).

During the next two decades, I visited the city several more times. With each visit I managed to experience a little bit more of what the city had to offer—I saw a Cubs game, rode the Ferris wheel at Navy Pier, and visited the Field Museum, the Art Institute of Chicago, and the Shedd Aquarium—and left after every stay knowing there was so much more to see and learn.

Finally, a couple of years ago I accepted a teaching job in Illinois. A large part of the reason I took it was that I really like Chicago. The new job wasn't in Chicago—in fact, it was pretty far from the

Windy City in terms of distance and state of mind—but it was only a three-hour train ride away. And a funny thing happened after I moved to the state: I not only continued to visit and find new things to experience in Chicago, but I started to learn more about Illinois. I learned the stories behind people I had vaguely known about, such as poets Carl Sandburg and Edgar Lee Masters, and heard more about familiar Illinois figures like Abraham Lincoln and Mormon Church founder Joseph Smith. I learned that the Underground Railroad passed through Illinois and that the first self-sustaining nuclear chain reaction happened beneath the West Stands of Stagg Field at the University of Chicago in 1942.

I discovered that Illinois had been ground zero for many events with national significance. Case in point: the seven debates in 1858 between Illinois senatorial candidates Abraham Lincoln and Stephen A. Douglas brought to the forefront the national discussion about the issue of slavery and were a prelude to their battle for the presidency two years later. Similarly, an 1894 walkout by Pullman Palace Car workers in Chicago cascaded into the first truly national labor strike. A tragic race riot in Springfield in 1908 helped create the National Association for the Advancement of Colored People (NAACP) a few months later. And then there was Disco Demolition Night at Chicago's Comiskey Park in 1979, a near riot by anti-disco music fans that marked the beginning of the end of the dance music's national popularity.

And because so many things of interest or importance have happened in Illinois, I know that I'll continue to learn about the state and will always have more questions—such as, Why are the Cubs such a big deal, anyway?

Just kidding.

Richard Moreno
Macomb, Illinois

JOLLIET AND MARQUETTE DISCOVER ILLINOIS

1673

It's difficult to imagine how explorers Louis Jolliet and Father Jacques Marquette felt when they paddled out into the broad expanse of the Mississippi River on June 17, 1673. For several years, French trappers and missionaries had heard rumors of a great river that flowed to the south. It was hoped that this river might be the legendary Northwest Passage leading to the Pacific Ocean, thereby opening a more direct trade route between Europe and China. The French government organized an expedition to search for the river and named Jolliet, a Canadian who had studied in France, to head the effort. He was joined by Marquette, a Jesuit priest who had learned six Native American tongues during seven years of missionary work with Canadian and North American tribes.

At the time they set off on their journey in two birch-bark canoes, Jolliet was twenty-seven years old and Marquette was thirty-five. They traveled with five boatmen and rations of smoked meat and Indian corn. The party departed on May 17 from St. Ignace (in modern-day Wisconsin) and traveled south on Lake Michigan to Green Bay. From there, they headed up the Fox River and then crossed overland to the Wisconsin River. The group followed the Wisconsin for more than a week until it merged with a much larger river—the Mississippi.

"Here we are, then, on this so renowned river, all of whose peculiar features I have endeavored to note carefully," Marquette wrote in his journal. "To the right is a large chain of very high mountains, and to the left are beautiful lands; in various places, the stream is divided by islands. On sounding, we found ten brasses of water. Its width is very unequal; sometimes it is three-quarters of a league [about two miles], and sometimes it narrows to three arpents (about 192 feet)."

For the next several weeks, the expedition traveled south on the Mississippi, encountering new terrain and fish, plant, and animal life. "From time to time, we came upon monstrous fish, one of which struck our canoe with such violence that I thought that it was a great tree, about to break the canoe to pieces," Marquette wrote in late June 1673. "On another occasion, we saw on the water a monster with the head of a tiger, a sharp nose like that of a wildcat, with whiskers and straight, erect ears." Marquette also recorded seeing and eating bison, which he called "wild cattle."

On June 25, Marquette wrote that the explorers came into contact with members of the Illini (also known as the Illinois and the Illiniwek) tribe. They spotted tracks on a well-traveled path on the shore, which he and Jolliet decided to follow: "Thinking that it was a road which led to some village of savages, we resolved to go and reconnoiter it. . . . Monsieur (Jolliet) and I undertook this investigation—a rather hazardous one for two men who exposed themselves alone, to the mercy of a barbarous and unknown people."

The encounter, however, went well, and the two sat down with representatives of the tribe and smoked tobacco pipes as a token of peace. Afterward, Marquette and Jolliet were invited to an Illini village, which scholars believe was most likely in Iowa, where they met a man that the priest called "the great captain of all the Illinois" and enjoyed a meal with him. Following the repast, the chief presented the expedition with a boy slave. The following day, the explorers returned to the Mississippi and continued heading south.

On the cliffs near the present-day town of Alton, Illinois, Marquette and Jolliet saw two large paintings of a horrible monster—later known as the Piasa Bird—that Marquette wrote "made us afraid, and upon which the boldest savages dare not rest their eyes. They are as large as a calf; they have horns on their heads like those of deer, a horrible look, red eyes, a beard like a tiger's, a face somewhat like a man's, a body covered with scales, and so long a tail that it winds all around the body, passing above the head and going back between the legs, ending in a fish's tail."

The party continued on the Mississippi for several days until they reached the mouth of the Arkansas River. There, they stopped and made contact with the members of the Quapaw tribe, who told them that they were only about a week away from the sea (Marquette believed it was likely the Gulf of Mexico), but that the Native Americans farther south were hostile. Marquette and Jolliet also saw European trade goods among the Quapaw and realized they would encounter the Spaniards if they continued south. Not wanting to be captured by either the Indians or the Spanish, they decided to turn back. The return journey was arduous because the group had to paddle against the river current.

In late August 1673, they reached the mouth of the Illinois River, which Illini tribal members had told them was a shorter route to Lake Michigan, and headed up that river. They came ashore at a spot near modern-day Grafton, Illinois, and in doing so became the first known non–Native Americans to enter what would become the state of Illinois. (Today, a large stone cross marks the place, which can be found near the entrance to Pere Marquette State Park.) A few weeks later, the group arrived at an Illinois tribal village called Kaskaskia, near the site of the modern-day town of Utica, Illinois. From there, they continued northeast to the end of the Illinois River and then traveled overland to the site of present-day Chicago. They paddled along the western shore of Lake Michigan back to Green Bay, where their expedition concluded.

Throughout their journey, Jolliet, who was a cartographer, had made maps and maintained a journal. While Marquette remained in Green Bay after the trip, Jolliet traveled to Montreal to share their discoveries. Along the way, however, his canoe overturned, and all of his records were lost. He did make an oral report of the trip, which was transcribed and sent to Paris.

Marquette, too, had kept a diary during the journey; when Jolliet's records were lost, Marquette's writings became the best account of the trip. A pair of manuscripts was made from Marquette's notes, but they were stored in a Montreal seminary for 150 years. An abridged version of the diary appeared in Melchisédec Thévenot's "Recueil de Voyages," which was published in 1681, but it wasn't until 1852 that an English translation of the complete manuscript was printed.

As for the two explorers, Marquette returned to his missionary work in the Illinois Territory in late 1674, and he wintered on the site of the future city of Chicago (becoming the first non-Indian to do so). In the spring of 1675, after celebrating mass before more than one thousand people at the Grand Village of the Illinois (near modern-day Starved Rock State Park), he suffered a severe bout of dysentery, which he had first contracted during the Mississippi expedition. He died while returning to St. Ignace.

Jolliet attempted to establish a French colony in Illinois but was denied permission by the regional government—apparently because he was too friendly with the Jesuits, who had fallen out of favor with the French government. He was, however, granted the Island of Anticosti on the St. Lawrence River near Quebec and later was made a minor lord in New France (Canada). He died in 1700 while traveling to Anticosti Island; his body was never found.

THE AMERICANS TAKE OVER
(THE BATTLE FOR KASKASKIA)

1778

By mid-1778, the war between the British and the upstart American colonists was badly stalled. In September of the previous year, the British had captured Philadelphia and, a month later, repelled an American counterattack at Germantown, Pennsylvania. Washington and his troops had barely survived the winter at Valley Forge. In February 1778, the French had signed a treaty with the Americans to supply troops, ships, and goods, and in June the British had abandoned Philadelphia to solidify defenses in New York. A major battle between the two sides at Monmouth Court House in New Jersey in late June had been inconclusive. The Americans badly needed a victory.

Enter George Rogers Clark. Born in 1752 in Virginia, not far from the home of Thomas Jefferson, Clark was one of five brothers who became officers during the American Revolutionary War. His youngest brother, William, was too young to fight in the war but years later became famous as one of the leaders of the Lewis and Clark expedition. By the time he was twenty-six, George Clark had earned a reputation as a solid military leader and was a major in the Virginia militia in Kentucky (at that time, Kentucky was part of the colony of Virginia). In 1777, the British commander at Fort Detroit had begun supporting efforts by British-friendly Native American tribes to harass and attack settlers in Kentucky. Clark decided that the best way to discourage the attacks was to capture British outposts north of the Ohio River. He was given permission by Virginia governor Patrick Henry to lead a secret war party to attack British strongholds in the area that would become the state of Illinois.

In July 1778, Clark and a small force of about 175 armed men crossed the Ohio at Fort Massac (near modern-day Metropolis, Illinois) and marched to the former French settlement of Kaskaskia, which had become a British outpost. He caught the British by surprise and, with the support of the community's French and Native American residents, who did not like the British, seized the city without firing a shot. He sent a messenger to the former French settlements of Cahokia and Prairie du Rocher (both in Illinois) as well as St. Phillip and Vincennes (in Indiana) and offered terms of surrender, which all accepted without resistance.

However, Lt. Governor Henry Hamilton, the Detroit commander, retaliated by mustering a force of British troops supplemented by friendly Indians, and they marched from Detroit to Vincennes. After recapturing the city, Hamilton released his Indian allies from service and hunkered down for the winter. His plan was to gather additional troops during the next few months and reclaim Kaskaskia and the other former British outposts that had been taken by Clark. Realizing his campaign would be a failure should Hamilton succeed, Clark countered by conducting a forced march with his men through swampy prairie lands. After covering about 240 miles, much of it wading through flooded areas and wetlands, Clark and about 172 militia members and volunteers again surprised the British when they arrived at Vincennes. Keen to keep the British off guard, he ordered his troops to hide behind a slight rise and had his flag bearers march back and forth so the British would believe his force was much larger than it was. After three days of fighting, Hamilton surrendered to Clark, who claimed the region for Virginia.

The victories in the region known as the "Old Northwest" were welcome news to Washington and the American troops fighting in the East. Historians have said that Clark's victories helped America persuade the French to enter the war on its behalf. Additionally, Clark's claim to the northwestern frontier lands cemented America's hold on the region, which encompassed much of what would become the Midwest. Those gains were formally recognized when the British ceded the area to the Americans in the Treaty of Paris in 1783.

Sadly for Clark, the victories at Kaskaskia and Vincennes were the highlights of his career. Following the war, Clark was named superintendent-surveyor of public lands granted to men who had served in the Virginia militia. In response to increasing hostilities between white settlers and Native Americans, Clark agreed to lead an expedition of 1,200 men against the Indians in 1786. The campaign disintegrated without accomplishing much when more than three hundred of the soldiers refused to continue in a dispute over supplies. It was also reported that Clark was often inebriated while on duty. He attempted to combat the claims by demanding a formal inquiry to clear his name, but his request was denied and Virginia politicians publicly rebuked him.

Additionally, since Clark had assumed personal financial responsibility for many of the expenses incurred during his various military excursions, and was not properly reimbursed by either the U.S. government or Virginia, creditors hounded him. Eventually, he lost most of the extensive land holdings in Indiana (about 150,000 acres) he had been granted for his role in the Revolutionary War. By 1803, his estate had dwindled to include a two-room cabin on a small plot of land in Clarksville, Indiana, overlooking the Falls of the Ohio, and a small gristmill that he operated with two slaves. In 1809, Clark, who was bitter about his treatment by Virginia officials and had become a heavy drinker, suffered a stroke, and as a result of an accident lost his right leg. Because he could no longer work his mill, he was forced to sell everything and moved to Locust Grove, Kentucky, to live with his sister and her husband. After suffering another stroke, he died on February 13, 1818.

Clark did ultimately regain much of his stature (and some of his fortune) in the years following his death. The state of Virginia finally repaid his estate for his war expenses (a lump sum of $30,000 and additional payments to his family until 1913). Additionally, in 1933, the federal government completed a memorial to him in Vincennes, Indiana, which is now known as the George Rogers Clark National Historical Park.

THE BLACK HAWK WAR

1832

When settlers began arriving in Illinois in increasing numbers in the late 1700s and early 1800s, it was only a matter of time before those who already lived there—Native American tribes such as the Illini, the Ho-Chunk, the Sauk, the Fox, and the Miami—came into conflict with the new arrivals. In response, tribes were presented with various treaties—some legal and some more questionable—designed, in most cases, to relocate the Indians. One of the most controversial was the Treaty of St. Louis, signed in 1804, which ceded all Sauk and Fox lands east of the Mississippi to the U.S. government.

Many of the Sauk and Fox, however, refused to recognize the treaty, which had been signed by U.S. President William Henry Harrison, because the Sauk and Fox representatives who had agreed to the terms of the treaty on behalf of the tribes were not authorized to do so. In particular, Black Hawk, a powerful Sauk war chief, opposed the agreement on the grounds that the proper tribal councils had not been consulted.

Not surprisingly, during the War of 1812, Black Hawk and a majority of the Sauk, Fox, and Ho-Chunk sided with the British against the Americans. The British promised Black Hawk that if the Americans were defeated they would create an Indian-controlled buffer and restore the boundaries of a previous agreement, the 1795 Treaty of Greenville. The result would have been to box in the Americans and limit future western expansion. Despite having repelled the Americans, who had started the war when they attacked Canada, the British were tired of fighting (they had also just defeated Napoleon's forces at Waterloo), and during peace negotiations they dropped their demand for the Indian buffer and ceded all western lands to the Americans.

In 1828, the U.S. government, citing the Treaty of St. Louis, gave the Sauk and the Fox one year to vacate all their lands in Illinois. By the spring of 1829, nearly two dozen white families prematurely settled on Indian lands at Saukenuk (Black Hawk's home village, which was located near modern-day Rock Island, Illinois) and in the process destroyed a number of Indian lodges and erected fences around the Sauk's farm fields. The Sauk tribe objected to the U.S. government but was ignored. In September a young Sauk chief, Keokuk, decided that it was best to avoid conflict with the whites and led most of the Sauk living on the east side of the Mississippi to the other side of the river.

In the spring of 1831, however, Black Hawk led a group of about 300 of his people back to Saukenuk and ordered the squatters to depart immediately. His warriors burned a number of cabins, and word spread that the Sauk had declared war on the settlers. Illinois Governor John Reynolds called up a militia of seven hundred men, later joined by about twice as many regular troops, which marched on the Indians. Faced with a much larger adversary, Black Hawk agreed to return to Iowa and signed a treaty promising not to return to Illinois without permission.

That winter, however, was a poor hunting season, and the Sauk did not have any suitable land for planting crops in Iowa (as they did near Rock Island). In April 1832, with his people starving, Black Hawk gathered five hundred men along with one thousand women and children and again crossed the Mississippi. He planned to plant corn with the Winnebago tribe near Prophet's Town, which was about fifty miles up the Rock River. Learning of Black Hawk's actions, Governor Reynolds again called up troops (including a young Abraham Lincoln, captain of the New Salem company), which this time numbered one thousand regulars and nearly two thousand militia members.

Meanwhile, Black Hawk tried to gain support from the other tribes to help fight against the advancing army. His pleas failed to persuade any to join him, so he decided to withdraw to Iowa. At a place known as Stillman's Run, Black Hawk sent a handful of braves with a white peace flag to a group of encamped troops, hoping to reach an agreement that would avoid bloodshed. He was under the impression that the troops, which numbered about 275, were under the direct command of General Henry Atkinson, leader of the Illinois army. The company, however, was a batch of newly recruited militia members under Major Isaiah Stillman. When the Sauk envoys reached the camp, the unruly militiamen attacked them, killing several. Black Hawk, who had brought about forty warriors with him, decided to counterattack and ordered his braves to charge the larger but disorganized group of militia members. The surprised soldiers turned and fled, providing Black Hawk with a psychological victory.

The rout, followed by several smaller successful attacks on settlers and the militia, emboldened Black Hawk but also spurred Illinois authorities to increase their efforts to put down the Indian uprising. In June 1832, a reconstituted army of about four thousand regulars and militia began a dogged pursuit of Black Hawk and his people through northern Illinois and into southwestern Wisconsin. In August, the army caught up with Black Hawk in Wisconsin for what became the final conflict of the Black Hawk War, the Battle of Bad Axe. There, the Sauk and Fox were soundly defeated, and, shortly after, Black Hawk surrendered. Defiant to the end, he said at the time: "[Black Hawk] has fought for his countrymen, the squaws and papooses, against the white men, who came year after year, to cheat them and take away their lands. You know the cause of our making war. It is known to all white men. They ought to be ashamed of it."

Following the end of hostilities, Black Hawk and several of his chiefs were taken to the eastern United States to be put in prison in Virginia and to meet with President Andrew Jackson and Secretary of War Lewis Cass. After being released from the prison, the captured Indian leaders were paraded through several American cities, drawing large crowds who were eager to view the exotic celebrities. Historians believe Cass sent the Indian leaders on the tour in order to impress upon them the size and resources of America.

After returning to Illinois, Black Hawk was held captive in Fort Armstrong near Rock Island, where he agreed to tell his story to an interpreter, Antoine LeClair, and newspaper editor J. P. Patterson. The result was a book, *The Autobiography of Ma-Ka-Tai-Me-She-Kia-Kiak, or Black Hawk,* which was the first Native American autobiography published in the United States. The Black Hawk War marked the end of major conflict between the Indians and white settlers in Illinois. The surviving Sauk and Fox, including Black Hawk, were sent to a reservation in southeastern Iowa; Black Hawk died there in 1838.

THE FIRST ABOLITIONIST MARTYR:
ELIJAH LOVEJOY

1837

Elijah Lovejoy didn't start out being an abolitionist. Or a minister. Or a martyr. Born in Albion, Maine, in 1802, Lovejoy graduated from Waterville College (now known as Colby College) in 1826 and moved to St. Louis to work as a scho+olteacher. Apparently growing bored with his job, Lovejoy acquired part ownership of a newspaper, the *St. Louis Times,* and became editor in 1830. At the time it was common for a newspaper to actively and strongly promote a particular political viewpoint, and the paper had an anti–Andrew Jackson/pro–Henry Clay slant that Lovejoy freely reflected in the paper's news stories and editorials. Lovejoy, however, was no ideologue on the slavery issue. His paper accepted advertising for slave sales, and he took on a slave as an assistant.

In 1832, however, Lovejoy attended a religious revival meeting and had an epiphany. He quit his job, enrolled in the Princeton Theological Seminary in New Jersey, and trained to become a minister. He returned to St. Louis in late 1833 and was ordained by the

Presbytery of St. Louis. He became pastor of the Des Peres Presby-
terian Church and began publishing a religious newspaper, the *St.
Louis Observer.* With the *Observer,* Lovejoy began to advocate the
elimination of slavery, which was a sensitive subject in St. Louis since
Missouri was a slave state that bordered Illinois, a free state.

Despite threats, Lovejoy continued delivering sermons and
publishing articles critical of the institution of slavery. According to
historian Robert P. Howard, "Amid growing hostility, he became
the unpopular champion of broad civil rights, including the right to
publish, to speak, to petition, and to assemble." He further incited
his opponents when he editorialized against a local judge for choos-
ing to dismiss charges against individuals involved in the burning at
the stake of a free African-American man. In response, a mob broke
into his newspaper office and damaged the printing press.

Concerned about the safety of his wife and son, in the summer
of 1836 Lovejoy moved across the Mississippi River to Alton, the
largest city in Illinois at the time and one that was perceived as more
progressive than St. Louis. Initially, Alton's business community
welcomed Lovejoy, who had become a bit of a celebrity. They also
believed he would moderate his views given what had happened in
St. Louis. But when he began the weekly *Alton Observer* in September 1936—on a new press—Lovejoy jumped back into the thick of
the slavery debate, calling it "an awful evil and sin."

During the next year, Lovejoy continued to publish frequent
attacks on the institution of slavery and called for the practice to be
abolished. In August 1837, a mob broke into the newspaper's offices
and destroyed the press once again. Lovejoy, however, was able
to continue publishing when he purchased a new press funded by
generous contributions from abolitionist easterners. About a month
later, however, another mob broke into the newspaper office and
threw the new press into the Mississippi River.

In response, Lovejoy and other like-minded abolitionists created the Illinois Anti-Slavery Society and announced plans to hold a public meeting in Alton to elect officers and set out goals. However, pro-slavery political forces led by Usher F. Linder, Illinois's attorney general, showed up in larger numbers than the abolitionists and subverted the meeting, electing pro-slavery officers and passing resolutions in support of the practice. At a follow-up meeting, a majority of those attending passed a motion asking Lovejoy to leave Alton.

In response, Lovejoy told the group: "I do not admit that it is the business of this assembly to decide whether I shall or shall not publish a newspaper in this city. . . . I know that I have the right freely to speak and publish my sentiments, subject only to the laws of the land for the abuse of that right. . . . You can crush me if you will; but I shall die at my post, for I cannot and will not forsake it."

Early on November 7, yet another new press arrived in Alton by steamboat. Lovejoy and his supporters quickly moved the equipment from the docks to a nearby stone warehouse, owned by a Lovejoy sympathizer. About fifteen of the group, including Lovejoy, armed themselves and prepared to guard the press with their lives. On the first night nothing happened, and the group hoped there would not be hostilities. However, on the second night, an armed and liquored-up pro-slavery mob of about 150 marched from the Tontine Tavern in Alton to the warehouse to demand Lovejoy give the press to them. The mob surrounded the building and shouted for the abolitionists to surrender. After a brief verbal volley, the mob began throwing rocks and firing shots at the men in the warehouse, who fired back.

A ladder appeared, which was propped against the side of the warehouse, and several men with torches began to climb with the intention of setting the building's roof on fire. Lovejoy and a couple of others ran outside and pushed the ladder down before safely returning to the warehouse. When the ladder was again put up,

Lovejoy and another man once again ran outside to push it over. Upon seeing the editor and his companion, several members of the mob fired upon them, hitting Lovejoy five times. Although badly wounded, Lovejoy managed to stumble back into the warehouse, where he fell to the ground, reportedly said, "My God, I have been shot," and died. Lovejoy's frightened supporters fled, which allowed the mob to finish its work and smash the new press.

Lovejoy's murder sparked a national outcry, particularly among antislavery and freedom-of-the-press advocates. Many described Lovejoy as the first martyr in the battle to eliminate slavery. Because of the nature of his death—protecting a printing press—some of those who had not yet chosen sides in the slavery debate began to see the potential threat that slavery presented to basic civil liberties. Ironically, many historians believe that Lovejoy's death served to energize antislavery forces rather than to silence them.

THE MURDER OF JOSEPH SMITH

1844

Joseph Smith feared for his life. Illinois Governor Thomas Ford had asked the founder of the Church of Latter Day Saints (Mormons) to turn himself over to the authorities in Carthage and assured him that he would be protected, but Smith anticipated the worst. The mood was ugly. Residents of Carthage had put out the word for anyone with a beef against the Mormons to come to their community. In nearby Nauvoo, the settlement that Smith and his followers had founded in western Illinois, there was talk of a holy war between church followers and nonbelievers.

It hadn't started out that way, however. In 1838, the Mormons had relocated to Illinois after being chased out of New York, Ohio, and Missouri. According to Illinois historian Annette P. Hampshire, Mormons were welcomed as "potential taxpayers and voters at a time of slow economic growth in the state." They purchased land in Hancock County in western Illinois and established a community they named Nauvoo, which meant, according to Smith, "beautiful place."

Within a few years, Nauvoo became the largest community in the state with more than eleven thousand residents (Chicago had 7,500 at the time). Thousands of Mormons and new Mormon converts arrived in the city from throughout the United States, Canada, and England. To accommodate the new community, in December 1840 the Illinois General Assembly approved a formal charter for the city, which established a city council as well as an independent militia known as the Nauvoo Legion.

From there, however, things began to go downhill. In November 1840, former attorney Thomas Coke Sharp had become co-owner and editor of the *Warsaw World* newspaper, published in Warsaw, Illinois, about seventeen miles south of Nauvoo. Sharp renamed the paper the *Warsaw Signal* and began publishing stories and editorials critical of the Mormons. According to Hampshire, "Sharp kept his readers informed of Mormon activities, and through his bitter editorials, he agitated for action against the church."

In particular, Sharp—as well as a number of longtime residents of the county—resented the growing power of the Mormons, who were starting to influence local and regional elections because they voted as a block (under the direction of the church's leader, Joseph Smith). In addition to editorializing against the Mormons, in 1841 Sharp called for the creation of an anti-Mormon political party. Tensions mounted in mid-1842, when a former Mormon Church leader, John C. Bennett, split from Smith and made claims in the local newspapers that Smith and other church elders practiced polygamy (marriage to multiple partners).

In June 1843, Smith was arrested while riding outside of Nauvoo by two deputies who tried to return him to Missouri, where he was still wanted for treason against the state. Members of Smith's militia, the Nauvoo Legion, intervened and returned him to Nauvoo, but his arrest was a sign that legal and political pressure on the Mormons was increasing. In response to Missouri's extradition attempt, the Nauvoo City Council passed a law authorizing the mayor, who happened to be Smith, to review any "foreign" legal paperwork issued from outside of the city and decide whether to honor it.

In June 1844, critics of the Mormons published the first issue of the *Nauvoo Expositor,* a newspaper with a clear anti-Mormon agenda. The paper stated its mission was to "explode the vicious principles of Joseph Smith, and those who practice the same abominations and whoredoms which we verily know are not accordant and consonant with the principles of Jesus Christ and the Apostles." The paper went on to claim that Smith was using religion as a pretext to bring innocent women to Nauvoo, where they could become part of his growing harem of wives.

Immediately after the newspaper appeared, the Nauvoo City Council met to discuss the threat the paper represented to the community. Smith persuaded the council to declare the newspaper a public nuisance and destroy its printing press. Later that same day, Mayor Smith ordered the city marshal to have the Nauvoo Legion carry out the orders.

Not surprisingly, the destruction of the newspaper incited anti-Mormon sentiment throughout the region. The *Quincy Whig* newspaper called it a "high-handed outrage." In his paper, Thomas Sharp wrote that he and other anti-Mormon forces were ready to "exterminate, utterly exterminate, the wicked and abominable Mormon leaders" and called for an assault on the city of Nauvoo. Providing legal cover, charges were filed against Smith and other Mormon leaders claiming they had promoted a riot. A constable was sent from the county seat in Carthage to Nauvoo to collect Smith, but he refused to comply. In response, anti-Mormon leaders sent out messengers to surrounding communities asking for armed men to come to Carthage to see justice done and take Smith into custody.

Faced with the prospect of an all-out war against the Mormons, Smith declared Nauvoo under martial law and mobilized the Nauvoo Legion (this action later resulted in his enemies filing charges of treason against him). Governor Ford learned of the impending conflict and on June 21 raced to Carthage to attempt to defuse the situation. He asked Smith to submit evidence justifying his actions against the *Expositor*. After reviewing the documents, Governor Ford wrote to Smith that his actions had been illegal and demanded he turn himself in to authorities in Carthage. He said that if Smith did not comply with the order, it appeared there would be an attack on Nauvoo.

Smith wrote back to the governor that he feared for his life if he left Nauvoo and said he wouldn't feel safe until the armed mobs in Carthage had dispersed. Believing that the situation was growing out of control, Smith and his brother, Hyrum, fled to Iowa to hide. He wrote to his wife Emma, asking her to bring his children and join him, with the intention of fleeing west. The letter alarmed Smith's followers in Nauvoo, many of whom felt that he was running out on the church at a time when it needed him most. Several church leaders persuaded Smith's wife to write him a letter urging him to return. Stung by the criticism, Smith and his brother headed back to Nauvoo and agreed to surrender to Carthage authorities. Despite Governor Ford's assurances that he and his brother would be safe, on June 24 Smith told his followers before leaving for Carthage, "I go as a lamb to the slaughter."

Upon arriving in Carthage, the Smith brothers spent the night in the Hamilton House, a local hotel where the governor was staying. The next day the two Smiths voluntarily surrendered themselves to the constable and were incarcerated in the prisoners' quarters on the second floor of the Carthage jail, a two-story stone building on the northwest side of the town. Justice of the Peace Robert Smith (no relation) ordered them committed without bail until June 29, when a material witness would be able to appear.

On the third day of the Smith brothers' incarceration, an armed mob appeared around the jail building. Late that afternoon, the mob broke into the building and rushed upstairs to where the prisoners were being kept. Hearing the commotion and shots being fired, the Smiths attempted to barricade the door. Members of the mob fired into the door, striking Hyrum Smith in the face and killing him instantly. Enraged, Joseph Smith, who had been smuggled a small pistol, opened the door and began firing into the crowd. After emptying the gun, he ran to the window, where armed men on the outside saw him and began firing.

Smith was struck four times: twice in the back, once in the right collarbone, and once in the chest. Mortally wounded, he fell from the second-floor window. According to several eyewitnesses, he was still alive after he fell and apparently "raised himself up against the well curb . . . drew up one leg and stretched out the other and died immediately."

Seeing they had accomplished what they set out to do and fearful of being arrested, the mob quickly dispersed. Upon hearing the news, the proprietor of the Hamilton House, Artois Hamilton, drove a wagon to the jail to secure the bodies, which he took to his hotel. The next day, the bodies were transported to Nauvoo, where they were eventually buried.

The murder of Joseph Smith marked the beginning of the end of the Mormon presence in Illinois. In the aftermath, church leaders wrestled with the issue of succession, particularly since Smith's brother had also been killed. In August of the following year, the church's ruling council selected Brigham Young as Smith's successor, despite claims by others that they had been chosen by Smith (or via divine inspiration) to lead the congregation. In 1846, continued harassment of the church by Illinois officials forced Young to lead his followers across the country to the Valley of the Great Salt Lake in Utah, where they established a more permanent home.

Today, Joseph Smith, Hyrum Smith, and Emma Smith are buried in the family cemetery adjacent to the Smith homestead in Nauvoo.

THE DONNER PARTY TRAGEDY:
IT ALL BEGAN IN SPRINGFIELD

1846

California sounded like heaven. Unlike Illinois or Ohio or Pennsylvania, where land was neither cheap nor plentiful, property in the western states like California and Oregon was said to be abundant, fertile, and virtually free. Starting in the early 1840s, hundreds of families began pulling up stakes in the eastern and midwestern states and headed west to seek better economic opportunities. Few, however, were prepared for the challenges they would face during the long journey.

Among those wanting to improve their station in life were George and Jacob Donner, two prosperous but older (George was sixty or, by some accounts, sixty-two years old, and Jacob was said to be about fifty-six) farmers from Springfield, Illinois, who had heard the tantalizing stories about California and decided to see if they could find their fortunes. Inspiring the Donners was a recently published book, *The Emigrants Guide to Oregon and California*, by Lansford Hastings, which described the wonders of the Golden State and briefly described a shortcut through Utah that could trim three hundred miles off the trek.

George Donner was born in North Carolina in 1786 and raised in Kentucky and Indiana. In 1828, Donner, by then a widower with five children, moved to Sangamon County, Illinois, where he established a farm about three miles northeast of Springfield. He married again and had two more children before his second wife, Mary, died. In 1839, he married Tamsen Dozier, a local schoolteacher, with whom he had three more children. The Donners soon owned two farms. They lived on one, which had eighty acres of farmland and orchards as well as a five-room, two-story house. Despite their relative prosperity, George Donner wanted more for his large family and decided he could find greater success in California.

Jacob Donner was also born in North Carolina, in 1790. While his brother George was described as a large man, about six feet in height, with a "cheerful disposition and easy temperament," Jacob was smaller in stature and less outgoing. Eliza Donner Houghton, George's daughter, described him as "a slight man, of delicate constitution, [who] was in poor health when we left Springfield, Illinois."

In the spring of 1846, George Donner placed a notice in the *Springfield Gazette* asking for able-bodied individuals interested in migrating west to join a wagon train that he and his brother were putting together. The Donners were soon joined by John Reed, a successful Springfield businessman who had also been planning to migrate to California to seek new opportunities.

John Reed was born in County Armagh, Ireland, in 1800 and had married Margaret Wilson Keys in Springfield in 1835. He has been described as a man with a strong personality, who was intelligent and energetic but also occasionally arrogant and overbearing. During the Black Hawk War of 1832, he had served with Abraham Lincoln and Stephen A. Douglas. In Springfield, the ambitious Reed operated a number of successful businesses over the years, including a sawmill and a furniture factory.

On April 14, 1846, the Donners and the Reed family set out for California from Springfield in nine wagons. At this point, the group consisted of George Donner, his wife, and five youngest children; Jacob Donner, his wife, and seven children; John Reed, his wife, and four children; and Reed's mother-in-law, Sarah Keyes. Additionally, the Donners employed two teamsters and brought along a friend, John Denton. A half-dozen employees, including three teamsters, accompanied the Reed family.

The group traveled to the official starting point for the Oregon Trail at Independence, Missouri, where they resupplied and began their journey. About a week later, they became part of a loosely organized cluster of some four dozen wagons heading west, led by William Russell. At this stage in the trip, a number of others joined the Donners and Reeds, including the Breen, Eddy, and Murphy families.

In late June, the wagons reached Fort Laramie, Wyoming, only about a week behind schedule. At Fort Laramie, the travelers received a letter from Lansford Hastings saying he would meet them at Fort Bridger and lead them on his shortcut, which passed south of the Great Salt Lake rather than going northwest to Fort Hall. Despite other reports saying that the Hastings Cutoff was not suitable for wagons, the group headed to Fort Bridger. On July 19, the wagon train reached Little Sandy River, the point where the trail split in two directions: north to Fort Hall or south to Fort Bridger. A majority of the group decided to take the safer, more known route via Fort Hall, but about twenty wagons, including the Donners and Reeds, continued to Fort Bridger. The group elected George Donner as its captain.

Unfortunately, by the time the Donner-led party reached Fort Bridger, Hastings had already departed. The group decided to continue on Hastings's trail and, after resting for four days, began the journey. Along the way, they gained a few additional members, which brought the total number of travelers in the Donner Party to eighty-seven people in twenty-three wagons. Despite reassurances that the Hastings Cutoff was a viable route, the party soon discovered that it was, indeed, barely passable. The wagon train had to cut its own road through large sections of Utah and Nevada, which slowed progress considerably. The members of the group were forced to abandon many of their belongings and some of the wagons along the way.

Tempers flared among the weary travelers, and in early October, following a disagreement, John Reed stabbed and killed John Snyder. The party voted to banish Reed; along with a man named Walter Herron, he rode off west. Reed's family, however, stayed with the main group. In mid-October, the wagons reached the Truckee Meadows (site of present-day Reno, Nevada). Nearly out of food, the group had sent several men ahead to Sutter's Fort in California to get supplies. Fortunately, shortly after the group stopped in the Truckee Meadows, one of the men returned with seven mules loaded with food and news that the route through the Sierra Nevada range was difficult but clear.

The exhausted party decided to rest for five days before making the final push into California. It would be a costly delay. On October 24, the wagon train began the climb into the mountains. Unfortunately, snow began to fall. And fall. About three miles from the summit (now known as Donner Pass) and blocked by five- to ten-foot snowdrifts, members of the party were forced to stop and make camp. Realizing they were going to have to stay for the winter, the various families built crude dwellings for protection, but there was little food. About sixty members of the party encamped near present-day Donner Lake, while the Donners and several others, who had traveled slower than the main group, constructed a camp about five miles lower down in the mountains.

As the weeks went by with virtually no food, seventeen members of the group made a desperate attempt to cross the mountains on snowshoes, but only seven survived. Meanwhile John Reed, who had crossed the mountains before it began snowing, tried to organize a rescue attempt from California. In February, a rescue party finally reached the stranded party and brought food. Twenty-three members of the group were chosen to return to California with the rescue group, including Margaret Reed and two of her children. In March, a second rescue party reached the group with food and evacuated seventeen members, mostly children. A third rescue party brought back four more, all children, but the last five survivors, most of whom were too weak to make the trip over the mountains, remained behind. In April, a salvage party arrived at Donner Lake to find only one person still alive and evidence that some members of the group had resorted to cannibalism to survive.

Out of the original eighty-seven members of the Donner party, only forty-eight survived the trip. Five died before the group became stranded in the mountains, while the other thirty-four died between December 1846 and April 1847 from starvation, malnutrition, the cold, or injuries. Of the original group that departed from Springfield, the survivors included six of the Donner brothers' children and all of the Reed family, except John Reed's mother-in-law, Sarah Keyes, who had died on the trail in May. In the two years following the episode, the number of emigrants traveling to California dropped to 450 in 1847 and 400 in 1848.

The following year—after the discovery of gold in California—the number jumped to twenty-five thousand.

ILLINOIS'S GREAT DEBATES

1858

The issue of slavery was growing more and more explosive. In 1854, U.S. Senator Stephen A. Douglas of Illinois had sponsored the Kansas-Nebraska Act, which created the Kansas and Nebraska territories and gave voters in each state the right to decide whether to permit slavery. As a proponent of a transcontinental railroad, Douglas saw the creation of the two territories as essential to ensuring the railroad would be built on a northern route, via Chicago. The act was seen as overturning the Missouri Compromise of 1820 and the Compromise of 1850, which had outlawed slavery above the 36°30' parallel. The act incensed the nation's antislavery forces, including a former Illinois congressman from Springfield named Abraham Lincoln, who shared the stage with Douglas at three public speeches during September and October 1854. At each, Douglas presented his arguments in favor of the act, and Lincoln would follow with a speech arguing against slavery and the act. The speeches were a prelude to a much more intense series of debates between Douglas and Lincoln four years later.

In June 1858, the newly created Republican Party of Illinois met in Springfield and selected Lincoln as its candidate for the U.S. Senate seat held by Douglas, a Democrat who was seeking a third term. Hoping to reinforce his bona fides against slavery, which most Illinoisans opposed, Douglas had opposed the Lecompton Constitution, a proposed constitution for the state of Kansas that would have allowed existing slave-owners to keep their slaves but prevented any new slaves from entering the state. Despite its being supported by President James Buchanan, also a Democrat, Douglas sided with antislavery politicians in Congress to defeat the proposed constitution. The end result was that Douglas gained the support of some slavery opponents but alienated a number of members of his own party.

Signaling his intentions, Lincoln's first speech after gaining his party's nomination was the famous "House Divided Speech," in which he paraphrased the Bible and noted, "A house divided against itself cannot stand. . . . I believe this government cannot endure permanently half slave and half free. I do not expect the Union to be dissolved. I do not expect the house to fall, but I do expect it will cease to be divided." The speech was seen by some as having too much of an abolitionist flavor, which might damage Lincoln's chances in the election.

Initially, the incumbent Douglas had an enormous advantage over Lincoln in terms of name recognition, visibility, and resources. In July 1858, Douglas appeared before a large crowd in Chicago to kick off his campaign and embarked on a whirlwind trip around the state on a special train. According to historian Robert P. Howard, Lincoln's campaign managers quickly realized that the only way to neutralize Douglas was to propose that he spend the remainder of the campaign debating Lincoln. Confident of not only his chances to win reelection but of his debating skills, Douglas accepted the challenge and agreed to seven debates in each of the congressional districts in Illinois that he had not yet visited.

The first debate was held on August 21 in Ottawa, fifty miles west of Chicago. Douglas came out swinging, claiming that Lincoln was a radical abolitionist who wanted to turn Illinois into a "free Negro colony." He said America had been half-slave and half-free for more than seven decades and questioned why that balance needed to be changed. He added that he was no supporter of slavery, but he also did not believe black people were equals of white citizens, and he opposed extending the rights of citizenship to them. He concluded by saying that each state should decide for itself whether it wanted slavery. Lincoln responded by denying that he, or his political party, were abolitionists and said he was content to keep slavery in the states where it existed but opposed its spread. He said slavery should be allowed to slowly die away.

The second debate, held on August 27 in the northern Illinois town of Freeport, saw Douglas continue to attack Lincoln. The latter successfully fought back when he asked Douglas if he believed the doctrine known as popular sovereignty—of which Douglas was a self-avowed champion—would allow residents of a new territory to vote to exclude slavery even before that territory became a state. The question had no easy answer. If Douglas answered negatively, it would imply that popular sovereignty was a sham and slavery could expand regardless of whether a state's residents wanted it or not. However, if he said "yes," Douglas would risk alienating voters in the southern states, who wanted to see slavery expanded into new regions. When Douglas responded in the affirmative, it reinforced the views of many southerners that Douglas was wishy-washy on the issue of slavery—and it was a position that two years later would come back to hurt Douglas when he ran for president.

At the third debate, conducted on September 15 in the southern Illinois community of Jonesboro, Douglas went on the offensive again, hammering Lincoln for his allegedly pro-abolitionist views and accusing his opponent of not only wanting to give blacks citizenship but also the right to vote and the right to marry white women. He also claimed that Lincoln was pandering to voters by saying different things in different parts of the state. Lincoln spent much of his time rebutting this charge and cited numerous examples of Douglas and the Democrats saying such things.

During the fourth debate, on September 18 in the eastern Illinois town of Charleston, Lincoln responded to Douglas's claims that he wanted to extend all rights to black people by, as Fergus M. Bordewich wrote in a 2008 issue of *Smithsonian* magazine, playing "his own race card." Lincoln said he was opposed to slavery, but was not for racial equality and did not believe the races were equal. "Ugly though it was, Charleston would prove to be the debates' turning point," Bordewich said, because it proved that Lincoln was tough enough to stand toe-to-toe with Douglas, who was viewed in the beginning as a far superior public speaker.

Debate number five was held on October 7 in the western Illinois hamlet of Galesburg, and it was there that Lincoln pressed his advantage in front of an overwhelmingly antislavery crowd. In this clash, Lincoln challenged Douglas's views on slavery using moral arguments. "Judge Douglas declares that if any community wants slavery, they have a right to have it," Lincoln said. "He can say that, logically, if he says that there is no wrong in slavery; but if you admit that there is a wrong in it, he cannot logically say that anybody has a right to do wrong."

The sixth encounter took place on October 13 in the Mississippi River town of Quincy. There, an ailing Douglas tried to rationalize his views regarding slavery by claiming that if slavery was not allowed to expand to other states, the naturally increasing population of slaves would soon outstrip the South's ability to support them and many of them would starve to death. Lincoln, on the other hand, said that while he did not support absolute equality for blacks, they should be allowed to enjoy the same right to life, liberty, and the pursuit of happiness as stated in the Declaration of Independence.

During the final debate, held on October 15 in Alton, near St. Louis, Lincoln returned to his theme of the immorality of slavery and said it was a threat to the country's high ideals and principles. Douglas, reportedly still so sick that his voice was difficult to hear, returned to personal attacks on Lincoln and the Republicans. In the end, many newspapers of the day generally felt that Lincoln had bested Douglas—largely by showing he could stand up to the better-known and more experienced senator when it came to debating and public speaking. Lincoln's eloquence in arguing against slavery also helped to make the issue one that would dominate the national scene for the next few years.

Despite his electrifying performance during the debates, Lincoln lost the Senate election. In those days, U.S. senators were elected by a vote of the state legislature, which, in Illinois, was dominated by Democrats. In the end, Douglas was reelected by a margin of 54 percent to 46 percent. In defeat, however, Lincoln gained national attention and was catapulted into the ranks of serious presidential contenders for the following election. In 1860, he became the Republican candidate for president and faced his old adversary, Stephen A. Douglas, who was the Democratic Party candidate.

That time, Lincoln won.

THE SINKING OF THE *LADY ELGIN*

1860

Captain Jack Wilson didn't like the way the sky looked. A veteran pilot on Lake Michigan, he knew that the open lake was no place to be during a storm. He thought briefly about canceling the journey, but decided to press ahead because his passengers were anxious to get home and he had a federal mail schedule to maintain. His ship, the *Lady Elgin,* had departed from Milwaukee late the night before, bound for Chicago. On board were some six hundred to seven hundred passengers (no accurate records were kept), many members of Milwaukee's Union Guard militia, which had organized an excursion to Chicago to hear a speech on September 7, 1860, by Democratic presidential candidate senator Stephen A. Douglas of Illinois.

Named after the wife of Lord Elgin, Canada's Governor General, the *Lady Elgin* was built in 1851 in Buffalo, New York, by Bidwell, Banta, and Company. A double-decked wooden side-wheel steamer, the *Lady Elgin* measured 252 feet long by 33.7 feet wide and rested in the water 14.3 feet deep. She was constructed of sturdy white oak with iron reinforcements and was designed to carry two hundred cabin passengers, one hundred deck passengers, a crew of forty-three, and about eight hundred tons of freight. Her normal route was between Buffalo, New York, and Chicago, Illinois, but she was also used for excursion trips across Lake Michigan.

The trip to Chicago had been uneventful. The *Lady Elgin* had arrived at her destination at about dawn on September 7. The members of the guard went on parade that morning and spent the day touring the city. That night many of the passengers attended a dinner-dance and heard Senator Douglas's speech. At about 11 p.m., nearly all of the passengers were back on the boat for the return voyage to Milwaukee. Captain Wilson reluctantly decided to forge ahead, and at about 11:30 p.m. the *Elgin* had cleared Chicago Harbor and was chugging into the open lake waters. Many of the passengers turned in for the night, but a few went to the ship's elegant salons to dance and enjoy the trip.

A few hours into the journey, the winds picked up and waters grew choppy. According to later reports, despite the gale-force winds, the *Elgin* was handling the storm well and making good time.

At about 2:30 a.m., when the ship was about seven miles off Winnetka, Illinois, the passengers felt the ship suddenly shudder and lurch to its port side. The *Elgin* had been struck by another ship, a schooner named the *Augusta,* which was carrying a load of lumber to Chicago. The *Augusta* had been flying most of her sails in the storm and was racing across the lake, nearly out of control. Focused on his ship's predicament, the *Augusta*'s pilot, Captain Darius Malott, did not notice it was careening toward the *Elgin* until it was too late. Before he could turn the schooner, it slammed into the side of the *Elgin* aft of its port paddle wheel.

Eyewitnesses said that just prior to the impact they had noticed the lights of an approaching vessel bearing down on the *Elgin*. The force of the collision caused most the *Elgin*'s oil lamps to extinguish, plunging the passengers into confusing darkness. The captain and the first mate, who were sleeping when the incident occurred, hurriedly dressed to check out the extent of the damage. Captain Wilson went below deck to find water quickly filling the engine room. Meanwhile, First Mate George Davis immediately determined that the ship was in danger and ordered the crew to turn it toward shore.

Aboard the *Augusta,* Captain Malott and his crew tried to quickly ascertain the extent of the damage to his ship. They looked for the *Elgin* and, not seeing the ship, assumed it had only received a glancing blow and had continued on its way. Concerned that his own vessel might sink, Captain Malott ordered the crew to continue sailing to Chicago as quickly as possible.

The crew of the *Elgin* tried to lessen the ship's load by tossing cargo and fifty head of cattle into the lake. In an attempt to lift the damaged side of the ship out of the water, the crew moved iron stoves and other heavy objects to the opposite side. A lifeboat was launched containing the first mate and a handful of crew members, but it drifted away because it had not been secured and contained no oars. Within twenty minutes of the crash, the *Elgin* began to break apart. Later reports noted that when the hull split, most of the passengers were on one side of the breach and the life preservers were on the other side. In response, crew and passengers grabbed anything that would float. As the ship sank, the ship's upper deck exploded. Within a short time, only debris, as well as the bow and two large sections of decking, upon which dozens of survivors had climbed, remained afloat.

An estimated five hundred of the seven hundred passengers and crew managed to grab hold of something to help keep them from drowning. As they drifted toward the shore, heavy rains, accented by flashes of lightning, pelted the survivors. Fortunately, the lake water wasn't so cold that survivors were in danger of hypothermia. The lifeboat reached the shore first. First Mate Davis climbed a steep cliff and reached the home of the Gage family, who were able to transmit word of the disaster to officials in Chicago. At about 8 a.m., a group of student volunteers from Northwestern University, who had heard about the catastrophe, arrived on the scene to help survivors.

Unfortunately, the stormy waters and the winds were generating huge waves and creating a strong undertow near the shore. As the survivors floated toward land, they were pummeled by the waves and dragged underwater. Those on the scene estimated that as many as four hundred people had managed to float to the shallow offshore waters, but more than half drowned in the treacherous surf.

There were tales of heroism. Captain Wilson made it to shore but drowned when he was smashed into some rocks while trying to help two women floundering in the surf. One of the Northwestern students, Edward Spencer, was credited with saving eighteen people. It was reported that he kept racing into the pounding waves, despite being continually battered by floating debris, to pull injured and exhausted passengers from the water.

For months following the disaster, bodies washed up on the shores of Lake Michigan. Of the more than four hundred confirmed dead, less than half of the bodies were ever recovered. Many of the bodies of the victims were so badly deteriorated that they were unrecognizable and were buried in a mass grave in Winnetka. A formal inquest in the months following the disaster found that both captains were not at fault and that the reason for the collision was a lack of proper navigation rules and procedures.

At the time, the sinking of the *Lady Elgin* and the loss of more than four hundred lives was the worst nautical tragedy to have occurred in Illinois. Sadly, that death toll was surpassed in 1915 when an overcrowded passenger steamer, the SS *Eastland,* rolled over while tied to a dock in the Chicago River, killing an estimated 844 people.

THE WINDY CITY BURNS

1871

If ever there was a place that had grown too fast, it was Chicago. Between 1833, when the city was formally organized, and 1871, Chicago had grown from fewer than one hundred residents to more than three hundred thousand. The city spread out over an area that was about six miles long and three miles wide. Because of its rapid expansion, much of the community was built of wood, including roadways that were surfaced with pine blocks and raised wooden sidewalks that kept residents from having to walk in the mud. In his book *The Great Chicago Fire,* Robert Cromie wrote, "the city of Chicago was virtually a cenotaph to the great northern forests lying beyond the far end of Lake Michigan. One of its features that would have struck an observer most forcibly was the fact that the city was built almost entirely of wood."

The summer of 1871 was unusually hot and dry. Records show that between July and October the city received about five inches of rain, which was about 25 percent of the normal amount. Chicago was a tinderbox city that only needed the smallest of sparks to set it afire.

That catalyst was a blaze that started in a barn behind the home of Patrick and Catherine O'Leary on the evening of Sunday, October 8, 1871. The O'Leary house, located at 137 De Koven Street on Chicago's West Side, was fairly typical for the lower-middle-class neighborhood. It was a modest wood-frame single-story cottage directly behind another small shingled house that the O'Learys rented out. Behind the O'Leary house was a barn in which the family kept five cows, a calf, and a horse. At about 9 p.m., Daniel "Pegleg" Sullivan spotted flames in the O'Learys' barn. Contrary to popular lore, Mrs. O'Leary was not in the barn at the time trying to milk one of her cows, nor did a cow kick over her lantern and start the fire—in fact, all of the O'Learys were already in bed for the night.

No one knows how or why the fire started, but when it did, Sullivan began shouting "Fire!" and tried to rescue the animals trapped in the barn. Another neighbor woke the still-sleeping O'Leary family, all of whom stumbled out of bed and scampered into the street. Patrick O'Leary and some of his neighbors began pouring water on the house to keep it from igniting. Embers from the burning barn were picked up by the hot, dry winds that were blowing through the city that night and carried to adjoining properties. Within a short time, the adjacent Dalton home burned down, and several other homes and barns had caught fire.

About ten minutes after the fire had started, a fire alarm was turned in by one of the neighbors, and the flames had been spotted by at least two local fire companies. A small hose cart arrived on the scene, but its crew quickly discovered their equipment was inadequate to extinguish the rapidly growing fire. A larger company, The Little Giant Engine Company, arrived and began fighting the fire. Unfortunately, other fire companies that could have helped contain the fire were sent to a wrong address by the dispatcher. By the time the fire companies were rerouted to the correct neighborhood, the flames had consumed much of the O'Learys' block.

According to Cromie, "the most crucial consequence of the spread of the fire was the increased heat, and with it the increased number of flying sparks, embers, and debris. The heat caused a powerful and ever-growing updraft, which in turn found an eager ally in the wind." Within hours, the fire had jumped the neighborhood and grown into nine separate fires burning a wide swath to the north and east. Flames jumped the Chicago River and blazed through the city's main business district and lakefront area. When city waterworks burned, firefighters found themselves without water and unable to halt the spread of the fire.

The conflagration finally dissipated on Sunday, October 10, helped immensely by the winds dying down and a light rain that had begun to fall. In the end, the fire destroyed an estimated $200 million in property. It burned an area that was about four miles long and averaged about three-quarters of a mile wide. About three hundred people died during the two-day inferno, which incinerated more than eighteen thousand buildings and left nearly a third of the city's residents homeless. Near Lake Michigan, 230-acre Lincoln Park was converted into temporary housing for about thirty thousand of the city's refugees.

Assistance quickly began to pour into the city. Several railroads offered to transport donated carloads of food and clothing at no cost from eastern cities to Chicago. The city of Cincinnati raised $160,000 for relief in only two days. Residents of New York, Milwaukee, and St. Louis sent trains loaded with food and other necessities. Illinois governor John Palmer called the State Legislature into a special session to appropriate money for relief. An estimated $4.8 million in relief funds was donated in the weeks and months following the fire.

The city began to rebuild immediately. By the end of the year, about six thousand temporary shanties had been erected along with two thousand more substantial wood-frame buildings and some five hundred permanent stone and brick structures. Chicago rebounded so completely that within two years of the disaster vacant property in the downtown business core was valued at more than the same land—including its building—had been worth before the fire. The city's most prominent businessmen, such as Potter Palmer, who lost an elegant new hotel, the Palmer House, and thirty-two other buildings, raised more than $3 million to rebuild. In the two decades after the fire, an estimated $316 million was spent on new construction in the city. The city's nearly vacant landscape became a blank canvas for some of the nation's most innovative architects, who introduced building techniques and styles that would influence construction all over the world.

Three days after the fire, *Chicago Tribune* publisher Joseph Medill wrote: "Let the Watchword henceforth be: Chicago Shall Rise Again." And she did.

THE BIZARRE PLOT TO RANSOM
ABRAHAM LINCOLN'S BODY

1876

Counterfeiter Big Jim Kennally simply had to get his best engraver, Benjamin Boyd, sprung from prison. Boyd, a very gifted artist when it came to creating fake money, had been picked up in October 1875 by federal Secret Service agents and sent to prison. Kennally and his crew desperately needed Boyd's talents if they wanted to continue their illegal currency operations. So Kennally concocted a bold scheme—what if someone were to kidnap the body of assassinated U.S. president Abraham Lincoln from its tomb in Springfield and trade it for Boyd's release from prison and some money?

In the summer of 1876, he sat down with several close friends in the Hub, a Chicago bar that he co-owned, and laid out his plan. He told the three men—Terence Mullen, his partner in the bar, Jack Hughes, who often passed counterfeit currency for Kennally, and Herbert Nelson, a local freight business owner—that he wanted them to break into the Lincoln Monument in Springfield, take the former president's body from its stone tomb, and secretly transport the coffin to the sand dunes on the Indiana side of Lake Michigan, where it would be buried. Next, he would surreptitiously inform Benjamin Boyd about the scheme and have Boyd contact the governor of Illinois to propose a deal: if he released Boyd and gave him $200,000 in cash, Lincoln's body would be returned unharmed.

Although there were obvious logistical problems, such as the fact that Springfield was a ten-day ride from the sand dunes at Lake Michigan and someone was bound to notice a coffin in the back of a strange wagon, the three men agreed to do it. Within days, however, Nelson backed out of the deal, and the other two were left scrambling to find a replacement. They settled on an acquaintance, Lewis C. Swegles, a local horse thief who frequented the Hub. Mullen and Hughes did not know that Swegles was also an informant for the Secret Service. Swegles, in fact, had been hired to report on the counterfeiting activities of Hughes and others involved in passing funny money.

In October 1876, Mullen and Hughes asked Swegles to partner with them in stealing Lincoln's body and holding it for ransom. After agreeing to help, a shocked Swegles immediately reported the plan to his Secret Service contact, agent Patrick Tyrell, who told Swegles to go along with the two but keep him informed. Tyrell quickly realized that Mullen and Hughes couldn't have concocted such an elaborate proposal and wanted to know the brains behind the plan.

In early November, Mullen and Hughes met with Swegles and outlined the plan. The three of them would leave by train for Springfield on November 6. The actual theft would take place on the evening of November 7—election night—when there would be few visitors at the cemetery and nearly everyone in Springfield, the Illinois state capital, would be watching the election returns.

After Swegles passed on the information to Tyrell, the agent put together a team to help him thwart the robbery. He recruited two other Secret Service operatives along with two Pinkerton detectives. He had also been in contact with Robert Lincoln, the only surviving son of the slain president, as well as John Todd Stuart, president of the Lincoln Monument Association. All had agreed that it would be better to catch the men in the act of stealing the president's body rather than arrest them beforehand.

That night, the would-be thieves as well as the Secret Service team boarded the same train for the overnight journey from Chicago to Springfield. Mullen and Hughes brought along a fourth man, Billy Brown, as a teamster to transport the coffin with Lincoln's body to the Indiana sand dunes. Brown, however, was really William Nealy, another informant for the Secret Service.

The next morning, Tyrell met with the custodian of the Lincoln Monument, John Carroll Power, to inform him about the details of the plot. That afternoon, Swegles and Hughes visited the monument, pretending to be tourists, and took a guided tour of the facility with Power. At about 8 p.m. that evening, all of the players were in position. Tyrell, Power, and the other agents hid inside the Memorial Hall adjacent to the tomb while Mullen, Hughes, and Swegles, who had walked two miles from their hotel to the cemetery, were outside reconnoitering the cemetery. Nealy was to come later with the wagon.

After seeing no one was around, Mullen and Hughes began filing through the padlock on the monument door (they first tried using a hacksaw, but the blade broke). They managed to cut the lock and opened the tomb. The three men removed the heavy marble lid on the sarcophagus and took off a marble panel at the foot of the large container. Once they had an opening, they tried to drag the double-layered lead and cedar coffin out but found it was too heavy. Mullen told Swegles to get Nealy, but the informant had walked straight to where Tyrell was hiding and whispered that it was time to take the grave robbers.

Tyrell quietly prompted his men, all of whom had taken their shoes off to minimize noise, to move in on Mullen and Hughes. One of his agents, however, cocked his pistol, and a few minutes later, as they were closing in on the tomb, it accidentally fired. The noise alerted the two thieves, who managed to escape. Not realizing that Mullen and Hughes were already gone, Tyrell and his men entered the tomb, saw the damage that had been done, and then fanned out to try to catch them. At one point, Tyrell saw a dark figure and fired a shot, which was returned by the man. After a few more shots were exchanged, the mystery man revealed himself to be one of Tyrell's own agents.

In the aftermath, Mullen and Hughes made it back to town and decided to head north on foot. Tyrell and his agents, along with Swegles and Nealy, returned to Chicago. A few days after the unsuccessful tomb robbery, Mullen and Hughes showed up in Chicago and headed straight to the Hub bar. Swegles reported their return to the Secret Service, which, on the night of November 17, arrested them without incident. The following day they were whisked to Springfield, and they were indicted a few days later. Legal maneuvering delayed the start of the trial until May 29, 1877. Two days later, a jury convicted the two of stealing a coffin—at the time there was no charge for trying to steal a U.S. president's body—and Mullen and Hughes were sentenced to a year in prison. The plot's mastermind, Big Jim Kennally, was never implicated in the crime, but he was arrested in 1880 in St. Louis for counterfeiting and sent to prison.

The attempted theft of Lincoln's body, however, did alarm Lincoln's friends and family. The two men most responsible for the monument, John Carroll Power and John Todd Stuart, both feared that smarter and better-equipped grave robbers might succeed where Mullen and Hughes had failed. They decided to hide the president's coffin in another part of the monument complex and not tell anyone.

On November 16, Lincoln's lead coffin was secured inside a wooden crate and buried in the basement of the Memorial Hall, underneath a pile of wood.

In 1878, the coffin was relocated to another part of the basement where the ground was drier. By this time, Power had recruited a handful of prominent Springfield businessmen, known as the Lincoln Guard of Honor, to help keep watch on the president's remains. When Mary Todd Lincoln died in 1882, members of the Guard secretly buried her coffin in the basement next to the president.

By the mid-1880s, Power had become convinced of the need for a more permanent and dignified solution. In 1887, the two coffins were unearthed, moved to a brick vault beneath the floor of the catacomb, placed inside wooden crates, and buried in cement. The new construction was impossible to hide from the public, and word soon spread about how the former president and first lady had been secretly hidden in the monument for many years. During the relocation, the Guard of Honor wanted to check on the state of Lincoln's remains and had the lead coffin cut open so they could view the body before it was reinterred.

About a decade later, custodians of the monument realized that the entire structure was in danger of collapsing. In 1884, a supporting arch had fallen, and water leaking into the foundations had destabilized the building. According to engineers, the only way to save the monument was to take it apart and reconstruct it on top of a new foundation built on bedrock. Additionally, the reconstruction would require digging up the coffins of President Lincoln and his wife yet again.

In 1900, workers broke through the cement and removed the two lead coffins (along with those of the Lincoln's three deceased children), which were transferred to new wooden crates and placed inside a temporary tomb that was covered with marble slabs and mounds of dirt. After reconstruction of the monument was completed in 1901, the coffins of President Lincoln and his wife were removed from the temporary tomb and placed inside a special vault that had been constructed ten feet below the floor of the catacomb chamber at the north end of the monument. The two caskets were secured inside wooden crates that were enclosed in a lattice of heavy steel bars. Tons of cement were then poured into the vault, ensuring that this would—at last—be President and Mrs. Lincoln's final resting place.

Today, visitors to Lincoln's Tomb can wander through the catacomb and view the vaults containing the three Lincoln children. An empty red granite sarcophagus stands in front of the place where the Lincolns are buried—ten feet below.

THE CHATSWORTH TRAIN DISASTER

1887

It had been an extraordinarily hot and dry summer. Newspapers throughout the state carried fire-danger warnings and noted that the cornfields were so parched there probably wouldn't be much of a crop that year. Against that backdrop, there were plenty of takers when the Toledo, Peoria, and Western Railroad (T. P. & W.) advertised a $7.50 round-trip excursion to the cool environs of Niagara Falls, New York.

On August 10, 1887, the Niagara Special, as the train was called, started out from the western Illinois hamlet of La Harpe filled with excited vacationers, some from as far away as Iowa. The train—pulled, ironically, by Engine No. 13—set out with about a dozen coaches and picked up additional passengers from the small rural communities along the route. In Peoria, a second locomotive and a handful of additional cars were added so that the train included some fifteen cars jam-packed with nearly eight hundred passengers. As the train, which was running two hours late, departed Peoria in the evening, passengers settled in for the long haul to New York.

It was about 12:45 a.m. when the Niagara Special left the small town of Chatsworth, located about seventy miles east of Peoria. Approximately two miles east of the community, the train began accelerating after it crested a small hill and started heading down a slope. At the bottom of the incline, the train, going an estimated forty miles per hour, crossed a small bridge. The first engine had just crossed the wooden trestle when it suddenly collapsed. The second locomotive turned onto its side and skidded into the ditch. The trailing wooden passenger cars slammed into the overturned engine as well as into each other.

According to the August 12, 1887, edition of the *Chatsworth Plaindealer,* the bridge had failed because it had earlier caught on fire and "the entire structure rested upon charred embers." The newspaper reported that the bridge "gave way, and in an instant the entire train, with the exception of the last four cars, was precipitated to the ditch, and many were instantly killed, not knowing what had occurred, while hundreds realized what had happened only as they found themselves crushed and wedged between heavy timbers, unable to move, with the dead and dying laying all around them. It was too horrible to admit of description. The screams and moans of the wounded were heartrending, and the terror of the sight cannot be imagined."

In the end, between eighty-one and eighty-five people perished and an estimated two hundred were injured in one of the worst train disasters ever to occur in Illinois. Seeing the damage, the crew of the locomotive, which had made it across the bridge, immediately steamed toward the closest community, Piper City, to get help while another crew member ran back to Chatsworth to seek assistance. Within hours, rescue crews and local residents were on the scene trying to help the injured and extract survivors. One of the most immediate fears was fire. While some of the wreckage did catch on fire, survivors and the first rescuers on the scene were able to extinguish the flames with dirt. Additionally, at 3 a.m. it began to rain heavily.

Many of the dead and the wounded were evacuated to Chatsworth, where several local buildings, including the T. P. & W. Depot, were temporarily converted into hospitals or morgues. The *Chatsworth Plaindealer* noted, "of the sixteen wounded left in Chatsworth, at this hour, eight are in private houses and eight on the upper floor of the Town Hall." Bizarrely, on August 12, 1887, the *New York Times* reported that many of the dead and injured had been robbed while still lying in the wreck, although that was not true. In the same story the *Times* also noted, "there is quite a general belief in Chatsworth tonight that the culvert fire was the work of an incendiary," but the rumor that someone had started the fire on purpose was also not true.

The *Times* went on to tell a handful of tales of great courage and tragedy. For instance, the paper wrote of a man named C. Felrath, who survived the crash relatively unhurt and went to help locate any other survivors. According to Felrath, he encountered a badly wounded woman in one of the mangled coaches who begged him to take her child to safety. Felrath said he took the baby and brought it to rescue workers but when he returned to help the woman she was dead. "Her last thought was for her baby," the *Times* said.

Another story in the *Times* involved a man named George Scott, who, although slightly injured, also helped with searching for survivors. Scott discovered a man with badly crushed legs who was being held in an upright position by heavy wooden timbers. The man was in such pain he implored Scott to provide him some type of relief or he would kill himself. After unsuccessfully trying to free him, Scott watched, horrified, as the desperate man pulled out a pistol and shot himself in the head.

An investigation following the crash revealed that a maintenance crew from the T. P. & W. Railroad had been in the vicinity of the bridge performing a series of controlled burns to prevent a brush fire from accidentally being started by floating embers from a passing train. According to a coroner's inquest conducted a week after the tragedy, on the day of the wreck the crew had set the grass around the bridge on fire, left it unwatched, and then went home for the day.

"The fire crept up to the end of the trestle works where there were a lot of old ties piled up to support the embankment," noted the *Peoria Weekly Journal* on August 25, 1887. "They smoldered away undermining the track . . . as soon as the train struck this the first engine passed over all right, but the next went down and the wreck followed."

A coroner's jury sought to hold the maintenance crew chief responsible for the deaths; he was arrested but the charges were soon dropped due to a lack of evidence. The exact cause of the accident was never officially determined.

PULLMAN'S FIGHT AGAINST FREE WILL

1894

George Pullman had always felt paternalistic toward his employees. In 1880, he purchased four thousand acres located about thirteen miles south of Chicago on the west shore of Lake Calumet and set out to build a perfect community for his workers. Pullman, Illinois, would be a model company town where his workers could live in clean, modern, efficient housing adjacent to an equally well-designed plant. The town would have sturdy brick buildings including a library, a four-story luxury hotel, a bank building, a school, indoor shopping areas, apartments, and an elegant church as well as expansive parks and dwellings that each boasted gas, water, and sewer service. His idea was to create a workers' utopia for his employees.

Pullman, born in New York in 1831, was the quintessential self-made man of the late nineteenth century. One of ten children, Pullman, who dropped out of school at the age of fourteen, was trained as a carpenter—he made coffins—by his father. In 1855, he relocated to Chicago because he saw economic opportunity in the city's need to lift many of its buildings when street grades were significantly raised. Chicago was located in a bog and the streets were thick with mud, making them nearly impossible to traverse at times. The soft, muddy soil meant that sewer drains had to be laid on top of the ground and covered. After this work was completed, the streets were six to eight feet higher than the foundations of the buildings.

Pullman, who had experience as a house mover, conceived of a way to slowly lift a building using hundreds of men and jacks. At his command, each jack supervisor would, in unison, turn the screw of the jack a quarter turn. The building would gradually rise above the foundations, which could then be rebuilt to the new height. The raising went so smoothly that many businesses didn't even have to close during the process.

With the wealth he earned from his building-raising business, the entrepreneurial Pullman decided to pursue a new venture—constructing luxury railroad cars. Between 1850 and 1860, the railroad business had exploded in the United States, connecting destinations that were farther and farther apart. Travel conditions, however, did not improve, so railroad passengers often complained of long, uncomfortable rides. Pullman's solution was to developing an upscale sleeping car with elegant trimmings, plush floor carpeting to muffle noise, and better suspension systems for a smoother ride. In 1864, the Pullman Palace Car Company was founded and quickly became the standard for comfortable rail travel in the country. In 1865, Pullman pulled off a public relations coup for his new car by using his connections to have President Abraham Lincoln's casket transported across the country in a Pullman Pioneer Car.

During the next decade, Pullman made his company into a success by constantly upgrading his products and introducing new railcar innovations, such as the dining car and the parlor car, where passengers could socialize together in comfort. One way that

Pullman ensured a constant revenue stream was that he leased his cars to the railroads rather than selling them to the companies. This arrangement allowed him to charge a premium for riding in his cars and to control the hiring of staff, including conductors and porters. It's estimated that by 1893, his company was worth more than $62 million (about $1.5 billion today).

According to Indiana State University history professor Richard Schneirov, Pullman was also a social innovator. He was one of the founders of the Young Men's Christian Association (YMCA) and a leader in the efforts to develop ways to encourage members of the poor and working classes to rise above their station in life to become members of the middle class. "To Pullman and others of his class the improvement of working-class character was key to social order," Schneirov said. "In their thinking, the ideal workingman would strive to ascend into the middle class through hard work, refraining from alcohol and associating with the saloon fraternity, and deferring immediate gratification in favor of saving for the future."

Pullman's ultimate solution was the creation of an ideal work-ingman society in the town that shared his name. But, as Schneirov noted, Pullman was no altruistic dreamer. He wanted to show that reform and capitalism could thrive hand in hand. His town would offer luxury, convenience, and cleanliness to the workingman but at what he deemed was a fair price.

The town was completed in about four years and Pullman quickly became an icon for enlightened business practices (at least as they were perceived in the 1880s). Visitors came from around the world to see how this model company town operated.

It wasn't long, however, before cracks began to appear in the town's shiny, happy veneer. Some workers resented the fact that Pullman would not sell homes to them but would only rent them to employees. Company staff also regularly inspected the homes to ensure they weren't being damaged. Additionally, Pullman rents were higher than those in surrounding communities, and he placed a 10 percent markup on city water and gas. Pullman's antialcohol beliefs—he only allowed booze to be served at his hotel—were another sore point. And there was resentment about the town's single church, which Pullman rented—again for a substantial fee—to any church groups for services. Most religious congregations wanted their own houses of worship and were not allowed to build in Pullman.

All of these factors, coupled with the fact that residents had no voice in how their community was governed, created a perfect storm for what became known as the Pullman Strike of 1894. The catalyst for the strike was the national Depression of 1893, largely sparked by overexpansion of the railroad industry. The resulting drop in Pullman's business caused him to cut employee wages by 30 percent. He didn't, however, reduce his rents or other expenses to those employees, arguing that he had promised those who had invested in the community a 6 percent rate of return. The pay cut seriously impacted many workers; some later testified that they were left with less than ten cents per month with which to feed their families after the company deducted expenses from their paychecks.

Against this backdrop, it was probably no surprise that workers went on strike on May 12, 1894. Immediately, the American Railway Union, of which most were members, agreed to back the strike. The union's leader, Eugene V. Debs, who later founded the Socialist Party of America, gave the Pullman Company five days to respond to the worker's demands for livable wages, but Pullman absolutely refused to negotiate. Reportedly, his response was to close his home, lock down the factory, and leave Chicago.

Faced with management that refused to bargain, Debs declared a sympathy strike on all trains carrying Pullman cars. This resulted in the shutdown of rail traffic in more than two dozen states between

Chicago and the West Coast. The plight of the Pullman workers became a rallying cry in Chicago, and many of its residents offered political support and encouraged charitable contributions to strikers. Debs had been careful to caution strikers to avoid any violence or property damage and to allow any trains carrying U.S. Mail to operate without impediment. He knew that should strikers interfere with the mail, federal troops would be called in to intervene on behalf of the railroad companies.

On the national level, however, President Grover Cleveland's attorney general Richard Olney, a former railroad attorney, viewed the strike unfavorably. In July, there was a violent clash in Blue Island, Illinois, during which striking workers destroyed railroad property. Shortly after, a federal court issued an injunction against the ARU and the strikers. Within days, federal troops were in Chicago, quelling the strike (an estimated thirty-four people died in clashes between troops and strikers) and forcing workers to return to their jobs.

While the strike failed, it is seen today as a sign of the increasing strength of organized labor in America. As for Pullman, the entire episode permanently damaged his reputation. A later presidential commission placed much of the blame for the situation on the industrialist for refusing to negotiate with his workers and placing undue economic hardships on them. When Pullman died in 1897, his family was so concerned that union sympathizers might desecrate his grave that they had him placed inside an eight-foot-deep pit made of steel-reinforced concrete, which was filled with more concrete and covered with asphalt.

DEATH PLAYS THE
IROQUOIS THEATRE

1903

The Iroquois Theatre was to be the safest, most beautiful, most cutting-edge performing arts facility in Chicago. Owners Will J. Davis and Harry J. Powers boasted in advertisements that the Iroquois was "absolutely fireproof." Located on Randolph Street between Dearborn and State Streets, the Iroquois was in the heart of the city's thriving theater district. To design the state-of-the-art theater, Davis and Powers hired a rising star in the local architecture world, twenty-eight-year-old Benjamin H. Marshall, who crafted a magnificent palace with an imposing facade that included giant stone pillars and a fifty-two-foot-high coved arch. Inside, the theater boasted a large and elaborately decorated foyer called the Grand Stair Hall and seating for 1,724.

Construction began in December 1902 and was—more or less—completed in mid-November 1903, just in time for a grand opening on November 23 and the busy Thanksgiving holiday season. In his book *Chicago Death Trap: The Iroquois Theatre Fire of 1903,* author

Nat Brandt notes that the project was plagued by delays and that the contractor, the George H. Fuller Company, was under considerable pressure to complete the job before the grand opening, which was postponed at least once.

To ensure the theater would draw customers, the owners booked popular entertainer Eddie Foy to perform in a new musical comedy, *Mr. Blackbeard.* The production, which originally played in London, was big; it boasted nearly three hundred performers, a stage crew of another two hundred members, and a forty-piece orchestra. The play was divided into three acts with eleven different scenes and required some 1,600 different costumes.

On November 23, while performers were rehearsing, workmen were still putting the finishing touches on the building. Opening night went smoothly. Brandt describes the audience, garbed in tuxedos and elegant evening gowns, as "a roster of Chicago's social elite." The local newspapers raved about the new theater, with the *Chicago Tribune* gushing, "The Iroquois is certainly unrivaled in perfection among the regular amusement places of the west, and it is doubtful if the east can boast more than one or two houses that are its equal."

The theater did solid business following Thanksgiving but really picked up during the Christmas holidays. As a result, the afternoon matinee performance on December 30 was completely sold out, and another two hundred tickets had been sold as standing room only. Since the show was perceived as being family-friendly, the audience included many children with their parents. Because of fears that people in the cheap seats might try to sneak into the more expensive seating, the theater manager closed and locked several accordion gates between the levels.

The first act went as planned. However, during the beginning of the second act, a hot-burning carbon arc lamp accidentally sparked, causing an adjacent curtain to catch on fire. Stagehands began trying to beat out the flames and tossed an extinguishing powder on the fire but were unable to put it out. An asbestos fire curtain designed to be lowered to protect the audience snagged on a lamp and failed to properly drop. Despite the rapidly growing fire, few in the theater immediately recognized the seriousness of the situation.

To prevent a panic, the orchestra continued to play and several actors stepped forward to try to calm the audience, which was beginning to grow restless. Meanwhile, stage-crew members and actors who were backstage began fleeing the theater. Most were able to get out of the building. Eddie Foy went out on the stage and urged patrons to stand and slowly vacate the theater in an orderly manner.

Unfortunately, once the audience caught sight of the smoke and flames, there was a rush to the exits. Many women and children were crushed to death in the ensuing chaos. Additionally, the locked accordion doors prohibited many on the upper floors from leaving the theater. According to later forensic reports, when the fleeing stage crew opened large freight doors at the rear of the theater, it created an air funnel that pushed the flames from the stage into the theater seats. The blast almost instantly asphyxiated hundreds of audience members. Additionally, when the plush, overstuffed theater seating caught on fire, it produced a thick, toxic smoke that killed many others.

In the end, an estimated 591 people, many of whom were women and children, died in the inferno—the worst building fire in American history. Fire investigators later discovered a host of safety violations that contributed to the disaster, ranging from a lack of exit signage to a dearth of operational firefighting equipment backstage. In one instance, an exterior fire escape didn't have a ladder to the ground attached to it, and in another instance a fire ladder became blocked by flames coming from a lower exit opening. Additionally, a large water pipe for a hose on the stage had never been connected (and the hose was missing). Large ceiling skylights that could have helped divert the flames away from the audience were inexplicably wired shut. While several members of theater management, including co-owner Will Davis, were arrested and indicted in the days following the fire, no one was ever convicted.

Chicago city officials, who had, after all, signed off on opening the Iroquois, moved swiftly to make it appear they were responsive to the disaster. Mayor Carter Harrison closed all the city's theaters and ordered each to remain closed until any safety violations found on that property were corrected.

As for the Iroquois, the structure did turn out, ironically, to be fireproof—the fire destroyed all the furnishings and the interior but did almost no damage to the walls. The owners rebuilt the facility and reopened it in 1905 under a new name, the Colonial Theatre. About two decades later, the Colonial was razed and replaced in 1926 by a movie house, the Oriental Theatre. In the early twenty-first century, the aging Oriental was renovated to become the Ford Center for the Performing Arts Oriental Theatre.

Today, there is no monument or commemorative sign at the site of the Iroquois to remember the victims. A memorial plaque that originally graced the lobby wall of the Oriental Theatre was apparently put into storage in the early 1970s and has been lost.

SPRINGFIELD'S RACE RIOTS

1908

It's ironic that the town of Springfield, Illinois, the state capital and hometown of the Great Emancipator, Abraham Lincoln, was also, in the summer of 1908, the site of one of the nation's worst race-related conflicts. Many historians, in fact, have had a hard time completely understanding why white rioters went on a rampage that resulted in the lynching and shooting of several blacks and the burning of a number of black-owned businesses and homes.

Some believe that the roots of the racial violence can be found in the fact that in spite of being Lincoln's hometown, Springfield, like many northern communities, had never been fully integrated. Black residents were restricted from eating in many restaurants, staying in many hotels, and socializing in many public places. Additionally, many of the community's brothels and gambling dens were concentrated in the poorest black areas, such as the downtown Levee district and an area known, appropriately, as the Badlands. Not surprisingly, these two neighborhoods also had the highest crime rates in the city. According to historian James L. Crouthamel, at the turn of the twentieth century Springfield "had a reputation, partly justified, of being one of the most corrupt mid-western cities. Vice was a business protected by the authorities and overlooked by respectable citizens."

Writing in the *Journal of Negro History* in 1960, Crouthamel suggested that the riots grew out of white frustration at corrupt municipal officials who allowed vice to flourish in the black areas and a general resentment toward southern blacks who were migrating in increasing numbers to northern cities, including Springfield.

The specific flashpoint for the rioting in Springfield was the allegation that a young black man, Joe James, had murdered Clergy A. Ballard, a white mining engineer, after Ballard had supposedly discovered James trying to assault his sixteen-year-old daughter in her bedroom. According to the reports, Ballard chased the assailant, who slashed him with a razor. The intruder fled and Ballard succumbed to his wounds a few hours later. However, apparently before he died, Ballard and his daughter identified James, a vagrant from Alabama, as the attacker. Police took James into custody after he was first grabbed by a mob and severely beaten.

About a month later, Springfield residents were shaken by newspaper reports of a second assault, this time involving a black man who allegedly raped a white woman. Police arrested George Richardson, who was identified by the victim as her attacker based on his voice.

The two crimes spurred calls for vigilante-style justice. On the evening of August 14, about four thousand people gathered around the jail that held both James and Richardson. Concerned about mob violence against the prisoners, authorities snuck them out of the facility and whisked them off to Bloomington. After discovering the two men were gone, the mob turned on local businesses, including a restaurant owned by Harry T. Loper (he was suspected of having helped remove the prisoners) and others in a nearby predominantly black neighborhood. According to Crouthamel, "The mob wrecked almost every building on Washington, Jefferson, and Madison Streets between Eighth and Twelfth Streets. It appears that the mob leaders were careful in destroying only homes and businesses which were owned by or served a Negro clientele."

By early the next morning, a large portion of the eastern end of Springfield was on fire. After looting local gun shops, some of the rampaging rioters began beating and shooting any unfortunate black person they encountered. Four white spectators were shot and killed by stray bullets. At about 2 a.m., the mob set fire to the home of Scott Burton, an elderly black barber. When he grabbed his shotgun to defend his house and fired into the crowd, he was shot four times and lynched from a nearby tree. As his body hung, vigilantes began to mutilate his corpse. They only stopped when a company of armed Illinois state militia appeared on the scene to restore order and cut down the body.

One of the mob's other victims was another elderly black man, William Donegan, whose only "crime" was that he had been married for more than thirty years to a white woman. The crowd found the eighty-four-year-old Donegan, who worked as a cobbler, sleeping in his backyard and quickly strung him up from a tree limb across the street from his house. Before he could die, someone slit his throat, and his body was hacked at with knives. The militia arrived to disperse the crowd and found he was still alive. He died in the hospital the next day.

By the next morning, most of the rioters had grown tired and gone home. By then, nearly four thousand state militia members from other communities had arrived in the city and set up camps in several places to maintain public order. "Springfield resembled a city in wartime on the morning after the riot, with squads of soldiers patrolling the streets, and entire battalions concentrated in the Negro area," Crouthamel wrote.

Not surprisingly, many of Springfield's black residents wanted to get out of the city. It's estimated that thousands left during the following days, most heading to Chicago or St. Louis (reportedly several Illinois towns, such as Jacksonville and Peoria, refused to allow them to enter city limits).

On the day following the riots, authorities rounded up about 150 people and charged them with various crimes. Three suspects— Kate Howard, Abe Raymer, and Ernest "Slim" Sullivan—were suspected of being the ringleaders for the worst of the mob violence and were quickly indicted by a grand jury. Additionally, Roy Young confessed to initiating the attack on Loper's restaurant and to starting a number of fires. In the subsequent trials, Raymer was acquitted on all counts and charges were dropped against Sullivan and most of the others. The only participant found guilty was Howard, who committed suicide by drinking poison before she could serve her time, and Young, who was convicted for burglary, arson, and rioting.

An interesting postscript is that George Richardson, who had insisted from the beginning that he was innocent of the rape charges filed against him, was completely exonerated when the alleged victim confessed that her assailant had, in fact, been a white man known to her, whom she had initially refused to reveal to authorities.

While the terrible events of August 14–15 soon receded from the general public consciousness, they did resonate among many early civil rights activists. On February 12, 1909, a group of reformers met in Springfield to discuss the creation of a permanent association of black and white activists devoted to protecting and safeguarding the rights of black Americans. Those in attendance included educators like Dr. W. E. B. DuBois as well as prominent social workers, religious leaders, and jurists. The result was the creation of the National

Association for the Advancement of Colored People (NAACP), which was incorporated the following year.

"Had the Springfield race riot not occurred at such an inopportune moment and at a place where the Lincoln aura was the strongest, the NAACP might not have been established," Crouthamel wrote. "Out of the violence at Springfield had come the organization of the first really effective Negro protest."

DISASTER UNDERGROUND:
THE CHERRY MINE TRAGEDY

1909

Saturday, November 13, 1909, began like most other days at the St. Paul Coal Company, Mine #2 near Cherry, Illinois. Between 6:30 a.m. and 7 a.m., nearly five hundred miners, some only teenagers, descended via a wobbly wooden cage elevator into the mine's inky depths. Because of problems with the mine's electrical system, there were no lights that day. In fact, there hadn't been electric illumination for weeks. As a result, the mine's tunnels were lit using kerosene torches, which were placed in notches in the mine's rough-hewn walls.

Laboring in an underground coal mine in the early twentieth century was especially dangerous work. In fact, the worst year on record for coal mine–related deaths in the United States was 1907, when underground fires, explosions, and cave-ins killed 3,242 men. In Illinois, commercial coal mining began in about 1810, when a small horizontal shaft was dug near Murphysboro in the southern part of the state. By 1907, Illinois had become the second biggest coal-producing state in the nation after Pennsylvania, its mines yielding more than fifty-one million tons of coal annually.

Mine #2 had been opened in 1905 by the St. Paul Coal Company to provide fuel to the Chicago, Milwaukee, and St. Paul Railway. Within a short time, the settlement of Cherry, named after James Cherry, superintendent of the mine, had cropped up adjacent to the mining operations. Many of the mine's workers were newly arrived immigrants from regions of modern-day Italy, France, Poland, Scotland, Austria, Ireland, Wales, and Slovakia. By 1909, the mine produced 1,500 tons of coal per day, making it one of the most productive coal mines in the state.

Shortly after noon on November 13, 1909, one of the mine's managers, John Bundy, ordered two workers, Robert Deans and Matt Francesco, to push a cart filled with a half dozen bales of hay to the mule stables on the second level. (Inside the mine were about forty mules, used to pull the wooden cars filled with coal.) As the two men neared the stables, they pushed the cart ahead and watched it come to a stop near a downward shaft. They turned and left, not paying attention to the fact that the hay-filled cart had come to rest directly beneath one of the torches. Kerosene began to drip onto the stacks of dry hay, which, a few minutes later, were ignited by a spark from the torch.

Initially, no one in the mine seemed particularly concerned about the blaze—apparently it wasn't unusual for small fires to occasionally break out because of the kerosene torches being used. By 1 p.m. the cart was on fire, but the miners who passed by, many of whom were taking an early leave because it was a Saturday, assumed the situation was under control. The two men most responsible for the fire, Deans and Francesco, were the first to report it to their superior, Alex Rosenjack. The three of them decided to try to extinguish the flames by pushing the car back and forth across the mine tunnel, apparently believing motion and air would blow out the fire. Unfortunately, all they succeeded in doing was spreading the blaze, as the overhead timber beams caught on fire. Next, they tried to shove the burning cart toward a sump or drainage area near the mule stables, but the fire was too hot. So they guided the car onto the wooden cage elevator, intending to lower it to a sump on a lower level. The cage, however, quickly caught fire. The men were able to lower the car to the lower level, where the fire was put out with a water hose used to wash the mules.

Despite having put out the cart and cage fires, the men were still faced with the fact that the support beams on the second level were now ablaze. Word of the fire did not spread because most of the miners were focused on their digging—not surprisingly, since coal miners were paid by the quantity of coal they removed, not by the hour. Deans, Francesco, and Rosenjack attempted to connect a hose to a water pipe closer to the fire but found the hose wouldn't fit on the pipe.

About forty-five minutes after the fire had started, the alarm finally went out to the miners to abandon the tunnels. The rush of men clogged the exits, and the mine began to fill with what is called "black damp," a toxic gas formed when coal burns in an environment that doesn't have enough oxygen.

Realizing that the mine was on fire, workers on the surface sounded the mine's emergency whistle, which attracted local residents eager to assist with the rescue efforts. The mine manager, John Bundy, organized a rescue team, which made several trips down the smoking main shaft to bring as many of the choking miners as possible to the surface. Using the cage was dangerous since it could catch on fire at any time, so rescuers dropped a ladder into the shaft and helped bring up a number of miners. However, the ladder soon caught on fire, leaving many miners trapped below the surface.

One of the mine's managers noticed that the giant fan that normally ventilated the mine was actually feeding oxygen to the fire. He reasoned that by reversing the fan he might be able to draw the flames away from the main shaft and the men. He ordered the big fan reversed, but that only made the wooden fan catch on fire when it sucked up the flames. He also didn't realize the fan had been the only thing feeding fresh air to the men in the mine, so its destruction worsened the situation for the men below.

A dozen men volunteered to take the cage down into the mine to attempt to save anyone they could locate. According to reports, the men dropped into the smoking hole six times, returning each time with a handful of miners overcome by smoke and heat. However, during the seventh trip down, the men began to frantically signal with a bell for the cage to be raised, but the operator didn't respond, thinking the signal wasn't the same as he'd heard during the previous trips. When he finally raised the cage, it was ablaze; all twelve of the heroic rescuers had burned to death.

The loss of the cage effectively ended any attempts to rescue the remaining miners. At 8 p.m., the mining company ordered the mine sealed so that the fire could be smothered. The order angered many of the miners' families and friends, who felt that the company had effectively condemned to death anyone who might still be alive in the mine. Many also believed the company was more interested in minimizing its property and equipment losses than in rescuing the miners.

On Sunday, a team from the Mine Explosion and Mine Rescue Station of the University of Illinois arrived with oxygen helmets, resuscitation gear, and special rescue tools. Two of the members attempted to be lowered into the mine to look for survivors, but they were soon thwarted by the intense heat and smoke. The mine was resealed. On Monday, the team made another rescue attempt but was again turned back by the underground inferno. Finally, on Thursday, after tons of water was poured into the shaft to try to extinguish the flames, firefighters climbed down into the mine to directly combat the blaze. By Saturday the fire was under control, and crews were sent down to remove the bodies of the dead.

Miraculously, a group of twenty-two miners had somehow survived the fire by digging into a cavern on a vein away from the main shaft. They erected a timber and mud barricade to keep out the toxic black damp and then, even more amazingly, discovered a small pool of water near a coal seam. The earthen barrier kept the poisoned air from reaching them, and for more than a week they subsisted on water as they waited to be rescued. On Saturday, one of the trapped miners became frantic from eight days of being confined to the small, subterranean chamber and pulled down part of the barrier. As he ran into the still-smoky, dark tunnel, he smashed his head into the low roof and was killed instantly. Four others decided to follow, hoping to get someone's attention. Fortunately, members of the cleanup crew heard their cries and rescued the surviving twenty-one miners.

Additional rescue efforts were halted when searchers found that some of the lower portions of the mine continued to burn, releasing deadly gases. On November 25, the mine was sealed and closed using steel and concrete. In the end, an estimated 259 men died in Mine #2. The accident triggered dozens of lawsuits, which the company tried to resolve with representatives of the miners and their survivors. A mediator worked with both parties to reach a settlement that resulted in awarding $1,800 to every family that had lost a primary provider. Many were outraged by the small amounts in the settlements, and the Illinois State Legislature responded by passing laws requiring not only better mine safety equipment but also establishing stronger liability standards that became the basis for the Illinois Workmen's Compensation Act.

THE EAST ST. LOUIS RACE RIOT

1917

In the late nineteenth and early twentieth centuries, booming industrial cities in the North and Midwest, like Chicago, Detroit, and St. Louis, were beacons of hope for African Americans seeking to escape the poverty and social shackles of the South. On the Illinois side of the Mississippi River, directly across from St. Louis, is East St. Louis. Like its neighbor, East St. Louis was experiencing rapid growth during that period. Many blacks found jobs there working in metalworking, at meatpacking plants, and for the railroads. The demand for such laborers became particularly acute in the years prior to World War I, and peaked during the war when many white workers left to serve in the military. According to historian Robert P. Howard, many East St. Louis companies actively recruited southern blacks to come to their community to help replenish the labor pool. By the spring of 1917, it was estimated that some ten thousand African Americans had relocated in recent years from southern states to East St. Louis.

East St. Louis was also a highly unionized, industrial community. Some companies encouraged the influx of largely nonunion blacks as a means of checking the power of the unions, which did not allow black members. Not surprisingly, this type of economic competition, coupled with racial tensions, was a recipe for conflict. On May 28 and 29, about three thousand union members marched on the mayor's office to demand East St. Louis companies fire their non-union workers, many of whom were black. After the meeting ended, some members joined into a mob that began destroying downtown buildings and beating any black citizens they encountered. Fortunately, no one was killed. Illinois Governor Frank O. Lowden called in the National Guard to restore peace to the community. Fearful of another attack, a number of black neighborhood associations were formed and vowed to protect their areas by any means necessary.

Things remained quiet during the first days of June, and the National Guard was ordered to depart the city on June 10. However, the community erupted again on July 1 after a car filled with white men drove through a black neighborhood and the car's occupants began randomly firing shots into houses, stores, and a church. While no one was hurt, many angry black residents armed themselves in order to defend their homes and businesses from any further aggression. When another car driven by a white man was mistakenly believed to be the same vehicle that had previously attacked them, a group of armed black men fired shots at the car, killing the driver and a passenger. Unfortunately, the second car had contained two police detectives sent to check on the earlier reports of shooting.

The next day, several thousand white residents gathered at a local labor hall and marched into the neighborhood where the shooting had taken place. A small armed mob, egged on by hundreds of cheering spectators, began attacking black people they encountered, regardless of age or gender. According to reports, black men and women riding on streetcars were dragged from the trolleys and beaten. By that evening, the rioters began burning black-owned homes and shops. Those attempting to flee were shot. There were reports of blacks being lynched on telephone poles and black children being thrown into fires. Called back to East St. Louis to contain the situation, National Guard troops were later said to have done nothing to prevent the violence and, in some cases, were alleged to have participated in the attacks. There were even stories of troops disarming black men and turning them over to the mobs to be beaten or killed.

When the rampage was over, at least thirty-nine black residents and nine whites (some believe the official numbers were low) had been killed, and hundreds were injured. More than two hundred homes and some four dozen businesses were destroyed. Rioters caused an estimated $3 million in damages. Historian Charles L. Lumpkins has described the riot as no less than an "American Pogrom"—a deliberate attempt to ethnically cleanse East St. Louis of its black residents in order to diminish rising black political power in the city. According to Lumpkins, the attacks were designed to force black residents to leave the city or stay but learn to accept their place in the local social order.

The riot triggered a massive exodus of black residents from East St. Louis. It's estimated that about seven thousand African Americans fled to St. Louis, and most never returned. The East St. Louis Riot has been called one of the bloodiest race riots in American history. Trials were held following the riot that resulted in the conviction of twelve black residents for murder (of the two policemen); nine whites were found guilty of homicide, and another forty-one whites were convicted of lesser misdemeanors. Of those, twenty-seven paid small fines and fourteen received brief sentences in the county jail.

There was a national outcry immediately following the riot. In a speech shortly after the event, former president Theodore Roosevelt condemned the activities of the rioters and called for a full investigation. On July 28, the National Association for the Advancement of Colored People organized ten thousand black people to march down Fifth Avenue in New York in silent protest. NAACP leaders demanded a federal investigation into the causes of the riots. Congressional hearings, conducted in East St. Louis from mid-October to mid-November, resulted in a report that blamed the rioting on the community's lack of a moral compass and showed how the business community, along with labor leaders and local politicians, were complicit in creating an environment where such an event could occur. No one, however, was ever indicted.

In spite of all the attention on East St. Louis in the aftermath of the riot, little changed during the next several decades. While segregation had been illegal in Illinois since 1885, the law was rarely enforced in East St. Louis. The city did not begin fully integrating restaurants, hotels, and schools until the mid-1960s.

THE HERRIN MASSACRE

1922

The *St. Louis Globe-Democrat* called the Herrin Massacre, a labor dispute that disintegrated into tragedy, "the most brutal and horrifying crime that has ever stained the garments of organized labor." The story of the massacre starts in the early 1920s, when the demand for coal was rising dramatically and southern Illinois contained the second-largest known coalfield in the country. Mining for the blue-black rock became just about the largest industry in many communities, particularly those located in Williamson County.

One of the towns located in the center of coal country was Herrin, a relatively young community (it was incorporated in 1900) of several thousand people. Most of the region's coal miners were loyal members of the United Mine Workers of America (UMWA), a labor union that had helped miners throughout the country obtain improved safety standards and working conditions and better pay. On April 1, 1922, the UMWA called for a nationwide strike in support of higher wages. Miners throughout the country, including coal miners in southern Illinois, walked off the job in support of the union's efforts.

About eight months before the strike was called, W. J. Lester of Cleveland, Ohio, had opened the Lester Strip Mine five miles from Herrin. Lester had incurred considerable debt in starting up his mine, so when the strike was called he negotiated with the UMWA to allow him to keep his mine operation open with the caveat that he wouldn't ship any coal to market. Lester planned to stockpile his coal and sell it quickly once the strike was over.

Not surprisingly, once the strike was in effect, the price of coal began to skyrocket. Desperate to repay his creditors—and, of course, realize a handsome profit—in mid-June Lester decided to ignore his agreement with the union and started shipping the estimated sixty thousand tons of coal that his workers had mined, worth an estimated quarter of a million dollars. To do this, he fired all of his union employees and imported fifty nonunion replacement workers and guards from Chicago.

Lester's actions enraged local miners. Further aggravating the situation was the fact that the armed men Lester had hired to guard his mine were rough and rude to locals. "One day strangers begin to appear in the town," *Time* magazine reported in a 1923 article about the events. "For a day or two nothing happens, and then the mine guards begin to patrol the highways. They search passersby, they frighten women, they boast and are hardboiled, as professional scabs and company detectives usually are."

The local union attempted to contact Lester to persuade him to honor his agreement, but he ignored their overtures. On the morning of June 21, several hundred miners gathered in the Herrin cemetery to hold an "indignation meeting" and voice their anger and frustration. Stirred up and eager to take action against the strikebreakers, a large group of miners and their supporters armed themselves—some with hunting rifles, others with weapons looted from local stores—and marched on the mine.

By about 3 p.m., the mob had surrounded the mine, and both sides started shooting at each other. The exchange of shots continued for nearly two hours and left two miners dead and several others wounded. Realizing they could not fight their way out, the trapped strikebreakers telephoned local authorities to beg for help. The mine's owner, Lester, was reached in Chicago and told about the situation. He agreed to close down the mine and honor the strike. In his book, *Bloody Williamson: A Chapter in American Lawlessness,* historian Paul Angle wrote that from about 4:30 to 6 p.m., authorities worked with the men trapped in the mine to negotiate the terms of surrender. It was agreed that all shooting would cease and each side would raise a white flag to signal they understood that a cease-fire was in place. At that point, Lester's nonunion workers and guards could exit the mine and be safely escorted out of the county.

The strikebreakers hung a white sheet over a telegraph wire and waited for the union workers to respond in kind. Unfortunately, a union representative sent to hang the other white flag arrived at the scene and did not see the sheet. Since he could still hear shots being fired, he decided the strikebreakers had reneged on the truce and departed. "Thus, as darkness fell, the best chance of peace slipped away," Angle wrote. Throughout the evening, additional armed union men from surrounding communities arrived at the scene.

Morning came with both sides still in a standoff. Finally, another truce was negotiated between the strikebreakers and the surrounding mob. According to reports, one of the guards, carrying an apron tied to a broom, told the union men that the men inside would surrender if they were allowed to depart unharmed. Believing a deal had been struck, at about 6 a.m. on June 22, the tired and scared strikebreakers surrendered to the mob.

A contingent of armed miners began to march the four dozen scabs toward Herrin. At Crenshaw Crossing, about a half mile from the mine, the group encountered additional union men, one of whom is said to have shouted: "The only way to free the county of strikebreakers is to kill them all off and stop the breed." Egged on by the newcomers, the mood of the miners escorting the men grew increasingly hostile. The group continued walking for another half mile before the mine superintendent, C. K. McDowell, who was bleeding from several head wounds and had an artificial leg, said he couldn't continue. One of the escorts grabbed McDowell by the arm and reportedly scowled, "I'm going to kill you and use you for bait to catch other scabs." With that, he and another man dragged McDowell about a hundred yards down a side road. Out of sight of the crowd, they shot the superintendent twice in the chest, killing him.

Now filled with bloodlust, the mob took the other strikebreakers into a nearby forest. They lined them against a fence strung with four strands of barbed wire and began firing. Those not killed instantly tried to climb over and through the fence. One man, who managed to avoid being killed at the fence, was caught in the woods and hanged. Six men escaped into the woods before being recaptured. They were told to remove their shoes and shirts and made to crawl to the Herrin cemetery. There, the six were tied together and members of the mob took turns beating and shooting them until they died (one who didn't die right away had his throat slit).

In the end, nineteen of the fifty strikebreakers were killed in the mob violence following the shoot-out. In the weeks after the affair, a Williamson County coroner's jury ruled that the men had been killed by unknown individuals and instead placed the blame on Lester and mining company officials for their acts leading up to the violence. The findings were soundly condemned in newspapers throughout the country and on the floor of the U.S. Senate, where Senator Henry Lee Myers of Montana described the killings as "anarchy pure and simple" and thundered: "What is worse than the commission of the crime itself is the fact that the united populace of the county where it occurred appears to approve of it."

In response to the national outrage, a special grand jury was convened in August to investigate the murders. Over the next several weeks, the grand jury heard testimony from witnesses and returned 214 indictments for murder, conspiracy, rioting, and assault to murder. The first trial was held in Williamson County in December and January, and resulted in not guilty verdicts for all of those charged. A second trial, held a few months later, also in Williamson County, ended in not guilty verdicts for all defendants. The State's attorney, Delos Duty, decided against proceeding with any additional trials, saying, "the prosecution is reluctantly obliged to admit that justice cannot be obtained in Williamson County."

State legislators conducted their own investigation. While a subsequent report criticized nearly everyone involved in the dispute, no formal action was ever taken, and no one was ever punished for the murders. With that in mind, it's perhaps not surprising that even today the county is sometimes referred to as "Bloody Williamson."

KILLER TWISTER

1925

The presence of tornadoes is a reality in the Midwest. Much like they were depicted in the 1996 movie *Twister,* tornadoes can be sudden, scary, and destructive. They're generally defined as a localized, violent windstorm that occurs over land, usually marked by a long, dark funnel-shaped column that occasionally touches the ground and destroys nearly everything in its path. Occasionally, a tornado can be deadly.

That was certainly the case on March 18, 1925, when, at about 1 p.m., a massive black vortex suddenly appeared near the small town of Ellington, Missouri, and began an unprecedented march of destruction across the states of Missouri, Illinois, and Indiana. Scientists later said it began when a low-pressure system from Canada drifted south, through Montana, into the Midwest. At about the same time, a moisture-filled front began angling north from the Gulf of Mexico. Somewhere over Kansas, the two slammed into each other, producing heavy winds and rain. While this didn't generate any reports of tornadoes in Kansas, as the storm moved east it grew in size and intensity.

"Just a few minutes into its life, the Tri-State Tornado [as it would later be called] had already established its three deadliest characteristics," wrote Peter S. Felknor in *The Tri-State Tornado,* an oral-history account of the deadly storm. "It moved at about sixty miles per hour, twice the typical forward speed of a tornado. The usual funnel cloud was, for the most part, not in evidence. And though it would cross mountains and plains and rivers and smash through town after town, nothing would sway it from the infernal bulldozer inevitability of its path . . . a swath of nearly complete destruction, often approaching a mile in width, for two hundred and nineteen miles."

The storm's first victim was a farmer who had the misfortunate of encountering the howling maelstrom of wind near Ellington. Within fourteen minutes of materializing, the force, which some described as a dark, amorphous rolling fog or a bank of roiling clouds, reached the small town of Annapolis, Missouri, where it killed another four people and destroyed 90 percent of the community. Racing along at more than seventy miles per hour, the storm sliced across the farmlands of northeast Missouri, ultimately killing between eleven and thirteen people, before crossing the Mississippi River and heading into Illinois.

The hamlet of Gorham, Illinois, was next. It was just before 2:30 p.m. when the tornado hit the town, uprooting trees and tossing houses and buildings about like toy structures. Within minutes the storm had passed, leaving behind thirty-seven dead (about half of the town's population) and a community entirely reduced to rubble. "The air was filled with 10,000 things," a St. Louis newspaper reporter later wrote. "A baby was blown from its mother's arms. A cow, picked up by the wind, was hurled into the village restaurant." From Gorham, the twister continued rapidly moving northeast toward the larger settlement of Murphysboro, which had a population of about twelve thousand.

It was in Murphysboro, where winds tore into the community at 180 miles per hour, that the storm did the most damage. According to the *St. Louis Post-Dispatch* newspaper, approximately one hundred blocks of the city were destroyed by the tornado and another seventy blocks were burned down in fires that started after the storm passed by. An estimated 234 people were killed in Murphysboro—the largest death toll in a single town struck by a tornado in U.S. history—and another 623 were injured. In addition to hundreds of homes, the twister wrecked the town's power plant as well as schools, churches, and dozens of commercial buildings. About eight thousand residents were left homeless. Perhaps most devastating was the fact that many of the industries destroyed by the tornado, including a shoe company, a silica plant, and railroad shops, were permanently lost—those businesses either relocated or didn't reopen. As a result, an estimated two thousand local jobs just disappeared overnight. "It completely changed my life," noted survivor Eugene Porter. "Many jobs were wiped out, so people had to leave town. It was almost like a war."

Sadly, that wasn't the end of the havoc caused by the storm. Five minutes after obliterating nearly half of Murphysboro, the tornado reached the small mining and farming town of De Soto. There, the winds flattened a substantial portion of the town, killing nearly seventy residents, including thirty-three children who died when their school collapsed. Photos of the town taken in the days after the disaster show a landscape that resembles a war zone, with piles of debris where homes and businesses once stood. From there, the mass of angry wind wiped out the small towns of Bush and Plumfield before reaching West Frankfort, which had a population of nine thousand. Many of the men in West Frankfort worked in local coal mines, so they weren't aware that the twister had struck until they lost electrical power underground. With the elevators not working, the miners were forced to climb up a shaft to leave the mine. Once they reached the surface, the men found parts of their city in ruins. The tornado had bypassed much of the business district, but it ravaged entire neighborhoods. In the end, 148 people died in West Frankfort and another four hundred were badly injured.

And the tornado marched on. At about 3:15 p.m. it struck tiny Parrish, population three hundred, where forty-six people were killed. Every building in the town was destroyed with the exception of a church, the schoolhouse, and one home. According to author Felknor, 541 people were killed during the forty-five-minute time period that the Tri-State Tornado had traveled through southern Illinois. The malevolent force continued heading northeast from Parrish, cutting a wide path through farms and fields of corn and soybeans, before crossing the Wabash River and entering Indiana. Once in the Hoosier State, the dervish careened into the village of Griffin, where twenty-five died, before hitting the communities of Owensville and Princeton. Then, as mysteriously as it had appeared, it disappeared. About sixteen miles east of Princeton, the seemingly unstoppable force of nature ran out of steam.

The death and destruction caused by the storm was staggering: 695 dead, 2,027 injured, and fifteen thousand homes destroyed. According to one estimate, the Great Tornado of 1925 caused more than $18 million in damage (in 1925 dollars). It had traveled 219 miles from where it appeared in Missouri to where it dissipated in Indiana, at an average speed of between fifty-six and seventy-three miles per hour. And it did all that damage in slightly less than three and a half hours.

THE WILLIAMSON COUNTY WAR

1926

The last public hanging in Illinois occurred on April 19, 1928. The man on the rope, however, was no ordinary thief or murderer. His name was Charlie Birger, and for many years he was one of the state's most notorious bootleggers and downstate gangsters. In fact, during the previous year or so Birger and his rivals, brothers Carl, Earl, and Bernie Shelton, had turned southern Illinois into a veritable battlefield, with each resorting to everything from aerial bombs to armored vehicles in a bid to wipe out the other. Ironically, a few years earlier Birger and the Sheltons had started out as bootlegging and gambling allies and had successfully defeated the forces of the Ku Klux Klan, which had sought to end the illegal liquor trade in the region.

Birger's story began in Russia, where he was born Shachna Itzik Birger in 1880. His family immigrated to the United States in the 1890s. After living in New York City for a brief time, the Birgers relocated to St. Louis, where Shachna, now known as Charlie, worked as a newspaper boy. After a few years in the U.S. Army and working as a coal miner, Birger bounced around the southwestern

Illinois area, eventually opening a successful roadhouse in Ledford that catered to local coal miners. After Prohibition began, Birger quickly became the kingpin of illegal gambling, liquor, and prostitution in the region. Handsome and affable, Birger also gained a reputation for being generous as well as violent.

In 1923, Birger killed a bartender named Cecil Knighton in a dispute over a woman. He was arrested but soon released after a coroner's jury ruled it was self-defense. However, a few days later he got into an argument with another man, William "Whitey" Doering, which resulted in a shoot-out between the two and several other associates. Birger was shot in the chest, and Doering was killed. In this instance, the coroner's jury ruled that it was difficult to determine who had fired the shot that killed Doering, and Birger was exonerated once again.

At the same time that Birger was expanding his reach, the Sheltons were establishing their own criminal empire in East St. Louis. According to Taylor Pensoneau, author of *Brothers Notorious: The Sheltons,* "It was inevitable that the Sheltons and Birger would meet, as the bigger fish surely do in a small pond." In the beginning, it was a friendly and mutually profitable relationship as they shared in the proceeds of nearly all of the bootlegging, gambling, and prostitution in the region.

The partnership flourished between 1924 and 1926, particularly when local anti-liquor forces brought in the Ku Klux Klan to combat the bootleggers. After an armed militia of Klansmen began raiding hundreds of roadhouses, saloons, and even private homes, there was a serious pushback by those who believed the Klan had gone too far, including bootleggers like Birger and the Sheltons. On February 8, 1924, anti-Klan forces, including Carl and Earl Shelton, met in Herrin to discuss ways to fight the Klan's efforts. When a couple of pro-Klan policemen tried to join the gathering, they were quickly disarmed. The angry mob, however, turned on the son of a pro-Klan constable, who happened to pass by, and killed him (Carl and Earl Shelton were later charged with shooting the man). Members of both the Klan and anti-Klan groups clashed in the streets of Herrin throughout the night, and the National Guard was brought in to restore order.

In January 1925, the leader of the Klan, S. Glenn Young, was killed in a cigar shop during a wild shoot-out with deputy sheriff Ora Thomas, part of the anti-Klan forces. In the following months, state officials managed to persuade both sides to accept a truce. The final blow to the Klan's efforts came in April 1926, when the Shelton-Birger forces decided to settle the issue once and for all on Election Day. For more than fifteen minutes, Shelton-Birger gunmen and armed Klan defenders fired at each other in the streets of Herrin. The two groups ended up fighting in front of the Masonic Temple polling place, where six men—three Klan supporters and three anti-Klansmen with ties to either the Sheltons or Birger—were killed.

In the aftermath of what became known as the Klan War, most of the surviving Klan leaders decided to leave the area. Without their interference, the bootleggers and gamblers began to expand their operations. Not surprisingly, however, the alliance between Birger and the Shelton brothers began to crumble when the Sheltons decided to move into his territory. Additionally, it was rumored that Birger had cheated the Sheltons out of their share of a slot machine operation they jointly owned. "Both the Shelton and Birger camps were emboldened by the ever present gunmen that each had enlisted to aid in the war against the Klan," wrote Pensoneau. "Going back to, or trying to enter, a normal life-style was difficult for many of these men who found staying available for murderous duty far preferable to holding a regular job. Some of these fellows had gotten their first taste of blood fighting the Klan. It was intoxicating. Even seen as glamorous. For them to turn next on each other was really only a natural progression."

By the late summer of 1926, the Williamson County War was on.

During the next five months, the two sides traded off murders, mysterious fires, and bombings. The Sheltons got creative and built what they called "the tank"—an old gasoline truck with the top of its rear storage tank cut off, which boasted a mounted machine gun. In response, Birger converted a Reo truck into an armored vehicle by covering it with sheet-metal plates. The two vehicles never met in battle, but their presence in the small towns and on the back roads of southern Illinois made a powerful and intimidating statement.

On November 10, a bomb was thrown from a passing car at the Shady Rest, Birger's main roadhouse, but missed its target. Two days later, the Sheltons tried again to destroy the Shady Rest by dropping several bombs on it from an airplane, but that effort also failed. In response, Birger, who was much more media savvy than the Sheltons, published in Harrisburg's *Daily Register* newspaper a statement assuring residents that those not part of the feud had nothing to fear and promised that no one "will be harmed in Harrisburg," which he said was his home and the place where he was educating his children.

That same month, the three Shelton brothers were arrested for orchestrating a mail robbery in Collinsville—charges pushed by Birger and his chief lieutenant, Art Newman, who both would testify against the Sheltons. About a month later, Birger was arrested for the murder of Joe Adams, the mayor of West City and a Shelton ally. The Sheltons were found guilty of the robbery charges, and each was sentenced to twenty-five years in prison (although they would be released after only a few years). In the 1940s, the Sheltons would move into Peoria, where they soon controlled most of that city's vice industries. In 1947, Carl Shelton, who had retired to farm in Wayne County, was shot to death by an unknown assailant, and a year later his brother Bernie was killed by a sniper outside of his office in Peoria. Neither killing was ever solved. After several attempts on his life, Earl relocated to Florida, where he died in 1986 at the age of ninety-six.

As for Birger, he had little time to celebrate his victory over the Sheltons. Following his trial for the Adams murder—he had hired the two men who carried it out, one of whom testified against him—Birger was sentenced to hang. While awaiting the results of his appeals, he watched the gallows being erected outside of his jail cell. On the day of his execution, the always-personable Birger shook hands with his hangman, Phil Hanna, looked at the crisp blue sky dotted with a few clouds, and reportedly said, "It is a beautiful world," before a heavy black hood and the noose were placed over his head. He died at 9:48 a.m.

SCARFACE GOES TO JAIL

1931

Throughout most of the 1920s, Alphonse Gabriel Capone, better known as Al Capone, ruled Chicago. As overlord of the Windy City's vice industry, he had his fingers in illegal activities ranging from gambling and prostitution to drugs and bootleg booze. He controlled the courts, the police, and the politicians. He was a larger-than-life figure who enjoyed living large. Yet it was something almost inconsequential—not paying his income taxes—that would finally bring down Chicago's colossus of crime.

Born in Brooklyn, New York, in 1899, Capone dropped out of school in the sixth grade when he joined the James Streeters, a tough local gang headed by Johnny Torrio that was part of the larger Five Points Gang that controlled the Lower East Side of New York. By 1915, Torrio had begun working in Chicago, helping his uncle by marriage, Big Jim Colosimo, who controlled a large chunk of the city's prostitution business. Four years later, Torrio brought Capone, who had earned a reputation as a reliable enforcer, to Chicago to help him move into the potentially lucrative business of bootlegging (the national prohibition on the production and sale of alcoholic beverages was to take effect in 1920). Torrio, however, couldn't persuade Colosimo to enter the liquor business. On May 11, 1920, Colosimo was allegedly gunned down by a Torrio associate from New York, Frankie Yale, but it could never be proven. In the aftermath, Torrio assumed control of Chicago's criminal enterprises, including gambling, prostitution, bootlegging, extortion, and racketeering.

Torrio, with Capone at his side, attempted to bring all of Chicago's main gangs into a unified confederation by dividing up the city and giving each gang an area in which it would operate without competition from any of the other gangs. The gangs, however, proved difficult to organize, and a war soon erupted between the North Side Irish gangs, headed by Dion O'Banion, and Torrio's forces. The battle culminated, in November 1924, with the shooting death of O'Banion and an unsuccessful assassination attempt on Torrio in January 1925. Despite being shot four times, Torrio recovered, but, perhaps wisely, decided to retire and turn all of the operations over to his chief lieutenant, Capone.

During the next few years, Capone methodically consolidated his power, eliminating or neutralizing any rivals. On February 14, 1929, he boldly attempted to wipe out one of his remaining competitors, the George "Bugs" Moran gang, during an event that has become known as the Valentine's Day Massacre. In a Chicago garage, shooters disguised as police officers machine-gunned seven members or associates of Moran's gang, and their leader narrowly missed becoming a victim himself. Although the murders were universally attributed to Capone, he was in Florida at the time. The brutal nature of the shootings focused national attention on Chicago's gangs, including Capone, and began a shift in public opinion against gangsters and their operations.

Ironically, it wasn't something big like murder or extortion that took down Capone; it was failing to file federal income taxes on his illegal earnings. In 1927, the U.S. Supreme Court ruled against a bootlegger who had filed no tax returns for several years—he argued that income from an illegal enterprise was not taxable and that to declare that income would violate the right against self-incrimination as defined by the Fifth Amendment. In its decision, however, the court said it could find no reason "why the fact that a business is unlawful should exempt it from paying taxes that if lawful it would have to pay."

The finding inspired Elmer L. Irey, chief of the Internal Revenue Service's Enforcement Branch, to go after Chicago's gangsters. After sending Capone's brother, Ralph, to prison for three years with a $10,000 fine for income tax evasion, he went after the head of the city's crime syndicate. Irey's team of agents decided to focus on Capone's 1925–29 earnings. In June 1931, a federal grand jury indicted Capone for income tax evasion for those four years, failure to file tax returns in 1928 and 1929, and conspiracy to violate Prohibition laws from 1922 to 1931. According to the IRS, which admitted it was only able to document a fraction of Capone's earnings, Chicago's top gangster had earned more than $1 million during those years and owed $219,260.12 in back taxes plus $164,445.09 in penalties. Capone faced a maximum penalty of thirty-four years in prison if found guilty of all of the charges.

Capone's attorneys immediately went to work trying to craft a compromise that would result in a lighter jail sentence. Federal prosecutors and the IRS agreed that if Capone would plead guilty to the twenty-three counts, they would recommend a sentence of two and a half years in federal prison. After reviewing the plea-bargain agreement for a month, judge James H. Wilkerson, who presided over the case, rejected the deal. Feeling betrayed, Capone immediately changed his plea to not guilty, and the case was scheduled for a jury trial on October 6, 1931.

For eleven days in October, jurors heard testimony about Capone's illegal operations and elusive income figures. After deliberating for only eight hours, they found Capone guilty of five counts of tax evasion and failing to file tax returns. A few days later, Judge Wilkerson sentenced Capone to eleven years in prison, $50,000 in fines, and $30,000 for court costs—at the time the stiffest sentence ever given to anyone for income tax evasion.

Not surprisingly, Capone's attorneys quickly appealed the conviction, but all of their attempts were ultimately dismissed. In May 1933, Capone was removed from the Cook County Jail in Chicago, where he had been imprisoned during his appeals, and was transported to the U.S. Penitentiary in Atlanta. A few months later, however, Capone was relocated to the government's new high-security prison at Alcatraz Island near San Francisco. Capone biographer John Kobler noted that Capone initially believed he would not be sent to the new facility, so when he was ordered out of his cell, "Capone went berserk. It took three more guards to drag him out of the cell."

For the next four years, Capone was more or less a model prisoner. He worked in the prison laundry room and generally avoided getting into trouble. On February 5, 1938, however, it became clear that something wasn't right with the mobster. That morning it was unseasonably warm, but he dressed in full winter gear, including a wool cap and his heavy peacoat, when he walked outside during a recreational break. He stood staring vacantly ahead and said nothing, even when spoken to by other inmates. Later, when he lined up for a meal, drool began to drip from his chin, and he vomited. Taken to the prison infirmary for observation, doctors concluded that Capone was suffering from advanced syphilis, which had affected his brain and central nervous system.

Capone spent another eleven months at Alcatraz, most of it in the hospital ward. When he was finally released from prison after serving only seven years of his sentence, he was a broken man, his body and mind ravaged by disease. The powerful gangster who once controlled one of America's largest cities lived for another eight years with only brief periods of lucidity. He died on January 25, 1947.

THE G-MEN FINALLY
GET THEIR MAN:
THE SHOOTING OF JOHN DILLINGER

1934

By 1934, John Dillinger had become more famous than most of the movie stars of the time. For a period of about fifteen months, Dillinger was one of America's most well-known outlaws. In addition to being named the Federal Bureau of Investigation's first Public Enemy No. 1, his larger-than-life exploits captured the imagination of a public reeling from the effects of the Great Depression and looking for a diversion.

Dillinger was a bank robber with not only bravado but also panache and style. During robberies, he was known to gracefully vault over bank railings, and some newspapers called him the "Gentleman Bandit" because of his politeness, particularly to women (he once offered his coat to a female hostage). When he was arrested for murder in January 1934 and incarcerated in the Lake County Jail in Crown Point, Indiana, he joked with reporters and posed for photos with his elbow playfully propped on the prosecutor's shoulder.

"This was something new," wrote Bryan Burrough in *Public Enemies: America's Greatest Crime Wave and the Birth of the FBI, 1933–34,* his 2004 book about Dillinger and the Federal Bureau of Investigation (FBI). "A headline-making criminal with charm, a bank robber who could crack wise on his way to the electric chair." Dillinger's ability to slip out of tight situations also contributed to his dashing image. Within a few weeks of his arrest in Indiana, Dillinger escaped from the Crown Point jail using a fake wooden gun.

Dillinger first gained notoriety in 1933, shortly after his release from prison—he had been arrested in 1924 for armed robbery and served a nine-year sentence. He joined several other men he had befriended in prison and began robbing banks throughout the Midwest. In September of 1933, he was arrested in Lima, Ohio, for an armed robbery he'd committed a month earlier. While he sat in jail, his confederates brazenly blasted their way into the facility, killing a sheriff, and freed Dillinger. During the escape, Dillinger stole the sheriff's car and drove it to Chicago, crossing from Indiana into Illinois. In doing so, he broke the National Motor Vehicle Theft Act—a federal offense, meaning the FBI could join the manhunt.

Initially, law enforcement officials, including the FBI, were unprepared to deal with someone like Dillinger. In November 1933, the Chicago police were tipped off that he was visiting a dentist and planned to nab him at the scene. When Dillinger exited the office, however, he quickly surmised that something was amiss and, after jumping into his car, managed to escape the police despite engaging in a brief but exhilarating shoot-out during a high-speed car chase. After his subsequent arrest and escape from the Lake County Jail in January 1934, Dillinger had another close encounter, this time with the FBI, in St. Paul, Minnesota, in late March 1934. There, an FBI agent and a local police inspector accidentally encountered Dillinger and an associate in an apartment where they were staying under assumed names. Once again, there was a shoot-out and the desperado managed to escape.

About a month later, the FBI again caught up to Dillinger, fellow gangster "Baby Face" Nelson, and several gang members hiding out in a rustic lodge called Little Bohemia in Manitowish, Minnesota. Despite being surrounded by agents, the outlaws eluded capture. Amid the chaos, FBI agents killed an innocent bystander and seriously injured two others, and Nelson killed an FBI agent during his escape. The entire episode was humiliating for the Bureau, which was openly mocked in the media for how it had bungled the arrests.

Meanwhile, Dillinger had come to realize that his face had become a little too famous—so he decided to change it. In May 1934, he found two doctors willing to perform cosmetic surgery on his face to make him less easily recognized. Telltale moles were removed, his chin dimple was filled in, and he was given a face-lift to eliminate wrinkles. After the incisions healed, Dillinger looked, in the words of Burrough, "like a new man."

By summer, Dillinger was feeling a bit more at ease and comfortable. He had a new girlfriend, a waitress (and, according to the FBI, a former prostitute) named Polly Hamilton, who roomed with a part-time madam named Ana Sage. Apparently smitten with Hamilton, Dillinger frequently took her to baseball games, nightclubs, amusement parks, the movies, and out to dinner. Hamilton later insisted she didn't know that the man who called himself "Jimmy Lawrence" was actually the notorious criminal John Dillinger. In July 1934, Dillinger moved in with Hamilton and Sage in an apartment at 2420 North Halsted Street in Chicago.

Hamilton may not have known Dillinger's identity, but Sage recognized the famous bank robber despite his attempts to change his appearance with surgery. On Saturday, July 21, Sage made contact with FBI agent Melvin Purvis, who had been chasing Dillinger for months. She promised to deliver Dillinger to the FBI, but she wanted something in return. Sage had been convicted several times for prostitution and for operating a brothel and was about to be deported to her native Romania. She told Purvis she would help authorities find Dillinger in return for his help in derailing her deportation. The FBI agent said he had limited authority in immigration matters but promised he would do everything he could to assist her if her information about Dillinger was true.

Sage told Purvis that she, Hamilton, and Dillinger had made plans to go to the movies the next night. She said she wasn't certain which theater they would be going to but promised to call Purvis when she had that information. She also said she would wear an orange skirt so agents could spot the three of them (she did not wear a red dress, as has been reported in some versions of the story).

The next day, Purvis organized a task force of about two dozen agents and local police officers and made plans to capture—or, if necessary, kill—Dillinger. At about 7:15 p.m., Sage called Purvis and told him that Dillinger and the two women would be seeing a film at either the Marbro or the Biograph theaters. While he had hoped to have more exact information from Sage, Purvis realized this might be his best opportunity to get Dillinger. He sent two agents to the Marbro while he and another agent waited outside the Biograph. His plan was to see where Dillinger went, assemble the full team of agents after the outlaw was spotted, and attempt to capture him when the movie was over. The signal for agents to move in on Dillinger would be when Purvis, standing outside the box office when the movie ended, lit up a cigar.

At about 8:36 p.m., as Purvis nervously waited in a car in front of the Biograph, the agent was startled to see Sage, dressed in orange, accompanying a pretty young woman and a neatly dressed man wearing a straw boater hat. As the film—*Manhattan Melodrama* starring Clark Gable—played, Purvis stationed his team at strategic points around the theater. At 10:40 p.m., Dillinger and the two women came out of the theater. Purvis, standing inches away from them, glanced at Dillinger and then lit his cigar. Incredibly, while some of the agents spotted the cigar and began to slowly move closer, several others missed the signal so Purvis was forced to do it again.

Afraid that Dillinger might escape, Purvis began to follow. Three agents who had seen the signal stepped in front of and beside Dillinger, who reached into his pocket for his gun and began to run away from the women. Almost simultaneously, the armed agents fired at Dillinger. According to a later autopsy, the famous criminal was struck four times: two bullets grazed him and another struck him in the side. The fourth, however, entered the back of his head and exited through his right eye, killing him almost instantly.

The FBI got Dillinger, but the woman who betrayed him, Ana Sage, still got deported. In 1947, she died of liver failure in Romania.

TALE OF TWO TRAGEDIES

1947 & 1951

Coal mining is not only a dirty business but also a dangerous one. While the Cherry Mine fire in 1909 remains the single worst mining disaster in Illinois history, a pair of underground catastrophes several decades later rank as equally tragic in terms of loss of life. The Centralia Mine disaster of 1947, which resulted in 111 deaths, and the West Frankfort coal mine explosion of 1951 (119 dead) showed that despite changes in mining regulations—many adopted as a result of the Cherry Mine fire—coal mining in Illinois in the mid-twentieth century wasn't much safer than it had been a half-century before.

The Centralia mishap occurred on March 25, 1947, when the Centralia No. 5 coal mine experienced a massive explosion that authorities later traced to an excessive amount of flammable coal dust in the air that was ignited by an unknown agent. Later investigators hypothesized that the deadly conflagration was started by either miners illegally lighting up a cigarette while on a break or a mechanical spark.

Perhaps the worst part of the Centralia fire is that it could have been prevented. For years, mine inspectors and miner's union officials had warned about an unsafe buildup of coal dust in the mine and recommended rock dust, which is pulverized inert rock like limestone, gypsum, or shale, be generously applied to places in the mine where the dust was thickest. Additionally, on several occasions the inspectors called for a water sprinkler system to be installed to dampen coal dust. Unfortunately, neither recommendation was followed by the mine's owners.

The day of the disaster had begun as a fairly typical Tuesday. At the start of the shift, about 140 men had descended the 540 feet into the mine to work the seams of coal. According to protocol, toward the end of the shift the mine's drillers and shot firers would prepare explosives to blast the coal from the rock walls. These would be detonated after normal mining operations had ended for the shift and workers were either headed toward the hoisting shaft that would take them aboveground or were already outside of the mine.

At about 3:26 p.m., as the miners were starting to head toward the exit shaft, the wax fuses, designed to provide ten minutes of lead time before igniting the dynamite, were lit. At about the same time, however, an explosion suddenly rumbled deep in the mine—too soon to have been one of the planned explosives. The blast ignited the coal dust that filled the mine. Within seconds, the explosion killed sixty-five men and dozens of others were injured and trapped. About fourteen men who survived the initial blast huddled in a room where they hoped rescuers would quickly find them. Sitting in the dark and realizing that the air was growing bad, they wrote brief notes to loved ones before they expired. During the next few hours, an additional forty-six men died from carbon monoxide poisoning. Twenty-three men managed to escape the mine and another eight were rescued.

The finger-pointing began almost immediately. The day after the disaster, Illinois's U.S. senator C. Wayland Brooks called for a formal investigation and the *St. Louis Post-Dispatch* editorialized, "the blood of the men who lost their lives in the mine disaster at Centralia is on the hands of the mine operators who continued to run the mine in the face of repeated warnings of an 'explosion hazard.'" John L. Lewis, the powerful head of the United Mine Workers of America, testified in Washington that the Centralia fire was an example of how federal mining authorities had failed to enforce proper safety laws and called on the four hundred thousand members of his union to mourn the Centralia dead with a six-day work stoppage.

The Centralia disaster was also commemorated in a May 1947 song by folksinger Woody Guthrie entitled "The Dying Miner (Goodbye Centralia)." In the lyrics, Guthrie captured the tragic final moments of many of the miners:

> *We found a little place in the air,*
> *Crawled and drug ourselves here.*
> *But the smoke is bad and the fumes coming in,*
> *And the gas is burning my eyes.*
>
> *Dear sisters and brothers goodbye,*
> *Dear mother and father goodbye.*
> *My fingers are weak and I cannot write,*
> *Goodbye Centralia, goodbye.*

Unfortunately, only four years after the Centralia fire, another southern Illinois coal-mining community, West Frankfort, was rocked by an equally tragic coal-mine disaster. On the evening of December 21, 1951, the New Orient Mine No. 2 experienced a deadly explosion. The cause was later determined to have been a buildup of highly flammable methane gas that was apparently ignited by a spark. Of the 257 men working in the mine at the time 119 died, most in the initial explosion, which was so powerful it snapped timbers in half, overturned loaded coal cars, tossed about heavy equipment, and nearly doubled-over steel rails. As at Centralia, several dozen died from carbon monoxide poisoning.

Rescue teams did find one survivor at the deepest levels of the mine, forty-four-year-old Cecil Sanders, who managed to stay alive despite being trapped underground for more than sixty hours. Sanders was said to have had enough carbon monoxide in his lungs to kill an ordinary man but, according to news accounts, he survived because he was very accustomed to the gas from having worked underground for so many years.

Within days of the explosion, John L. Lewis was on the scene along with Oscar Chapman, secretary of the U.S. Department of the Interior, and John Forbes, director of the U.S. Bureau of Mines, to inspect the mine and offer assistance. Chapman announced he was opening a federal investigation into the tragedy, and Lewis used the occasion to push for stronger federal mine safety regulations, including improved ventilation standards. In the aftermath of the explosion, president Harry S. Truman signed into law the Federal Coal Mine Safety Act of 1952, which improved controls on coal dust, required better ventilation in underground mines, and empowered mine inspectors to shut down mines that don't comply with the standards.

Of course, it was small consolation to the 105 wives and 161 children left behind.

CHICAGO'S BIG SHOW TRIAL

1969

The 1968 Democratic National Convention was going to be Chicago's chance to shine in the national spotlight. The Democrats hadn't met in the Windy City since 1956, when Illinois native son Adlai Stevenson had been nominated for president (he lost to Dwight D. Eisenhower). Chicago's mayor, Richard J. Daley, who had been elected in 1955—and would serve until 1976—saw the convention as an opportunity to show off his city as an orderly, safe, and friendly community that rivaled any other major metropolitan area in America.

But there were bad omens. The year 1968 was filled with turbulence and tragedy. That year, the Vietnam War became the longest war in U.S. history up until that time, and opposition to the conflict, which had already claimed more than thirty thousand lives, was growing. Democratic president Lyndon Johnson, who escalated America's involvement in the Vietnam War, had become deeply unpopular because of his war policies. In March, he dropped out of the presidential race, throwing his support behind his vice president, Hubert H. Humphrey. In April, Rev. Martin Luther King, a prominent civil rights activist, was assassinated in Memphis. In June, senator Robert Kennedy, one of the strongest contenders for the Democratic Party nomination for president, was killed on the night he won the California primary.

Against this backdrop, several antiwar groups, including the National Mobilization Committee to End the War in Vietnam (MOBE), Students for a Democratic Society (SDS), and the Youth International Party (Yippies), decided to conduct a youth event called Festival of Life in Chicago at the same time as the Democratic National Convention. The idea was to bring thousands of young antiwar protesters into the city during the convention to show their opposition to the war and to conventional American values. According to Douglas O. Linder, a law professor at the University of Missouri–Kansas City who has written about the 1968 convention and subsequent events, the groups came together despite having differing goals. He said the MOBE and the SDS were mostly interested in protesting the war in a nonviolent way, while the Yippies wanted to mock the status quo, promote a counterculture lifestyle, and question authority.

Mayor Daley, however, wanted nothing to do with protesters disrupting the convention in his city. When the antiwar groups filed for permission to demonstrate in the city and to be allowed to sleep in city parks, Chicago city officials denied the requests and imposed an 11 p.m. curfew. The mayor decided that a big show of force would discourage protesters, so he put the city's 12,000 police officers on twelve-hour shifts and stationed another 7,500 Army troops and 6,000 National Guard members around the city to maintain order.

On Sunday, August 25, activists and protesters began to trickle in for the kickoff of the Festival of Life in Lincoln Park. The day progressed relatively peacefully, with young people handing out flowers, smoking pot, listening to poetry, and frolicking. However, at about 10:30 p.m., police surrounded the park, and an officer announced on a bullhorn that the park would be closing and anyone who tried to stay would be arrested. The message was met with jeers and a few thrown objects. At 11 p.m., police moved into the park, firing tear gas at those who had lagged behind and clubbing others with their batons. Within a few hours, the park had been emptied.

The following night saw a similar scene. About three thousand demonstrators gathered in Lincoln Park, and just after 11 p.m. police began wading into the crowd with their clubs and firing tear-gas canisters. That was followed by two more days of marches and speeches to increasingly larger crowds during the day followed by violent clashes with police and arrests each evening. Journalist Haynes Johnson, who was covering the convention for the *Washington Star,* later wrote, "the violence that rent the convention throughout that week, much of it captured live on television, confirmed both the Democrats' pessimism and the country's judgment of a political party torn by dissension and disunity."

By Thursday, the convention was over, and the protesters began to dissipate. Mayor Daley pressed for charges to be brought against protest organizers and, in March 1969, a Chicago grand jury returned indictments against eight demonstrators as well as eight police officers. The eight leaders of the protesters—Abbie Hoffman, Jerry Rubin, David Dellinger, Tom Hayden, Rennie Davis, John Froines, Lee Weiner, and Bobby Seale—were charged with conspiracy to cross state lines to incite a riot, teaching the making of an incendiary device, and committing acts impeding police in their lawful duties.

The subsequent proceedings, popularly known as the Chicago Seven trial (Seale's case was soon severed from the others), became a grand circus. The trial judge, seventy-four-year-old Julius Hoffman, was the former law partner of Mayor Daley and had a reputation for being an irascible, no-nonsense judge. When defense attorneys submitted a list of fifty-four questions for jurors that might assist the attorneys in determining bias, Hoffman tossed out all but one of them. As a result, the jury that was selected was overwhelmingly white, middle-aged, and middle-class.

During the trial, Judge Hoffman did little to hide his contempt for the defendants, who resorted to increasingly outrageous behavior to show their disdain for him and the entire trial. Before his case was removed from the group, Seale was ordered bound, gagged, and chained to a chair because he had called Judge Hoffman "a pig, a fascist, and a racist." At one point, Yippie leader Abbie Hoffman told the judge he was "a disgrace to the Jews. You would have served Hitler better"; both Davis and Rubin loudly told the judge the proceedings were "bullsh-t." During the five-month trial, Judge Hoffman issued more than two hundred citations for contempt of court against the defendants and their attorneys.

Not surprisingly, the jury found five of the seven defendants guilty of intent to incite a riot while crossing state lines; Froines and Weiner were found not guilty of all charges. During sentencing, Judge Hoffman sentenced each of the defendants and their defense lawyers to long prison terms on 159 charges of criminal contempt. He then sentenced the five defendants to the maximum sentences: five years in prison and a $5,000 fine. Additionally, seven of the police officers charged with violating the civil rights of demonstrators were found not guilty, and the charges against the eighth officer were dismissed.

In 1972, however, the Seventh Circuit Court of Appeals threw out all of the convictions, citing Judge Hoffman's refusal to allow the defense attorneys an opportunity to determine the cultural biases of the potential jurors. The court also condemned what it described as Judge Hoffman's "deprecatory and often antagonistic attitude toward the defense."

It would be twenty-eight more years before the Democratic National Convention was again held in Chicago.

DISCO INFERNO

1979

It seemed like a good idea at the time. Chicago disc jockey Steve Dahl, the morning host at radio station WLUP-FM ("The Loop"), hated disco music. A year earlier he had lost his job at another radio station, WDAI, when it had switched to an all-disco format. After he was hired at The Loop, he had embarked on an on-air anti-disco crusade that had included the live smashing of disco records during his program as well as creating and airing parody songs of popular disco hits. He had even formed an anti-disco "army" of his fans, called the Insane Coho Lips.

In the summer of 1979, he had a brainstorm—why not create an event to, in his words, "end disco once and for all"? Working with his cohost, Garry Meier, his radio station, and Mike Veeck, the promotion-minded son of Chicago White Sox owner Bill Veeck, he came up with Disco Demolition Night. On July 12, during a doubleheader between the White Sox and the Detroit Tigers, fans would be allowed entrance to the games if they paid ninety-eight cents (WLUP's frequency was 97.9) and at least one disco record.

During the intermission between the two games, the collected vinyl discs would be piled on the field and blown up.

"I thought it was going to be a failure," he told the *Chicago Tribune* in 2009 upon the thirtieth anniversary of the stunt. "Even if I drew 10,000 fans, the place would have still looked empty. I was just hoping I wouldn't be too embarrassed. I mean, I was dressed up like a fat G.I. Joe, singing 'Do You Think I'm Disco' (a parody of Rod Stewart's disco hit 'Do You Think I'm Sexy') a capella and running around blowing up records."

The promotion attracted an estimated sixty thousand fans to Comiskey Park, the forty-four-thousand-seat home of the White Sox. Another ten thousand fans were turned away at the gate. The turnout was astounding considering that the Sox were a mediocre team that year and rarely filled their stadium on Chicago's South Side. Apparently, many of those in attendance weren't the typical baseball fans that usually came to Sox games but were there specifically to show their support for Dahl and their hatred for disco music. "I remember from the get-go, it wasn't a normal crowd," Tigers shortstop Alan Trammel told the *New York Times* in a 2009 article about the event. According to news accounts of the day, the stadium was festooned with "Disco Sucks" banners, and many in the crowd were intoxicated or stoned.

The trouble began before the first game started when some of those in attendance began tossing vinyl records in the stands. In *Roctober,* a music magazine, writer Steve Mandich noted, "apparently it occurred to none of them [the event's promoters] that records are fun to throw, capable of slicing through the air like Frisbees, only with much greater distance and velocity." Tigers player Rusty Staub told the *Times* that the flying vinyl records "would slice around you and stick in the ground . . . It wasn't just one, it was many. Oh, God almighty, I've never seen anything so dangerous in my life. I begged the guys to put on their batting helmets."

Despite the increasingly unruly crowd throwing records, cardboard album covers, beer cups, and any other type of projectile onto the field, the groundskeepers and batboys were able to quickly remove any trash, and Detroit won the first game 4–1. When the intermission started, a giant green wooden crate filled with thousands of disco records was transported out to center field. Dahl appeared, dressed in a military-style jacket and a green helmet, and made his way to the box. After riling up the crowd with chants of "Disco Sucks," he announced he was ready to get on with the destruction. After a brief countdown, several Roman candles burst from the ground in front of the crate filled with the disco records. That was followed by a loud explosion as the container was blasted into a whitish cloud of flying album covers and shards of vinyl records.

Unfortunately for the White Sox, that wasn't the end of the fireworks. Shortly after the explosion, a handful of rowdy spectators climbed out of the stands and ran out onto the field. Within minutes, several thousand out-of-control fans had hopped the fences and were running around the baseball diamond waving their anti-disco banners, ripping up the bases, throwing records, and lighting the field on fire. Baseball players who were warming up on the field saw the rampage and quickly raced to the safety of the clubhouse and dugout. According to reports, the batting cage was torn down and dragged across the field. One fan grabbed a high-pressure water hose and began spraying water all over the outfield while others ripped out chunks of the grassy field. News accounts estimated more than seven thousand fans participated in the riot.

Despite public-address messages calling for people to return to their seats—including by legendary Sox announcer Harry Carey, who tried unsuccessfully to lead the crowd in a rendition of "Take Me Out to the Ballgame"—the anarchy continued for more than thirty minutes. The overwhelmed stadium security forces were unable to regain control of the situation. Finally, Chicago riot police arrived at the stadium. About eighty police armed with batons and shields lined up and began marching in unison toward the crowd. At the sight of the officers, most of the mob climbed back into the stands. Within five minutes, the police had restored order and arrested thirty-nine people for disorderly conduct. The stadium groundskeepers attempted to clean up the mess, but after an hour the second game was called because the field remained unplayable. The next day, the league announced that the Sox would forfeit the second game because the team had been unable to provide an acceptable playing field.

Ultimately, Disco Demolition Night did achieve what Steve Dahl had wanted. The event is generally viewed by music historians as more or less marking the beginning of the end of the disco music fad. In his 2004 book *The History of Rock and Roll,* author Thomas E. Larson said that 1978 was the start of a backlash against disco music, particularly by hard-rock fans. Larson cited Disco Demolition Night as the seminal moment in the anti-disco movement and wrote, "by 1980, disco was not only a dirty word, it was dead."

POISON PILLS

1982

Someone poisoned and murdered seven people in the Chicagoland area in the fall of 1982. Between September 29 and October 1, seven individuals died after taking over-the-counter Extra-Strength Tylenol capsules that had been laced with toxic potassium cyanide. The tragedy resulted in a national recall of the popular pain-relief medicine and the creation of tamper-proof packaging for medicines in the United States. Yet despite a national manhunt by state and federal law enforcement officials, the case has never been solved.

The first victim in the so-called Tylenol Murders was twelve-year-old Mary Kellerman of Elk Grove Village, a suburb of Chicago. According to news reports, Kellerman, a seventh grader, awoke early on the morning of September 29 with a sore throat and a runny nose. Her parents gave her a single Extra-Strength Tylenol capsule, which she dutifully swallowed with water. By 7 a.m., she had collapsed on the bathroom floor. She was immediately taken to the hospital, where she was pronounced dead. Perplexed doctors initially believed she had died from an unexpected stroke.

That same day, Mary Reiner, twenty-seven, who lived in the Chicago suburb of Winfield, had a slight headache and took two Tylenol capsules. She, too, immediately became sick, was rushed to a hospital, and died a few hours later. Unfortunately, those weren't the last related fatalities of the day. In Arlington Heights, located north of Chicago, postal worker Adam Janus took two Tylenol and collapsed in his home. He died shortly after in a nearby hospital emergency room of what was initially believed to have been a massive heart attack. While working in a telephone store in a shopping mall in Lombard, thirty-year-old Mary McFarland went to the break room to take a couple of Tylenol for a bad headache. After she collapsed and died, her doctors thought she had suffered an aneurysm. That evening, Adam Janus's family gathered in his home to absorb the shock of his sudden death. His brother, Stanley, twenty-five, and Stanley's wife of three months, Theresa, nineteen, had headaches and took a few Tylenol from a bottle they found in his home. Stanley died that evening; Theresa died two days later.

It was the symptoms of Stanley and Theresa Janus that provided investigators with their first clue that the deaths were somehow related. When the two were rushed to Northwest Community Hospital, the attending physician, Dr. Thomas Kim, began to suspect that something wasn't right. Their symptoms were unusual—very low blood pressure and diluted pupils—and they did not respond to any treatment. He contacted the Rocky Mountain Poison Center in Denver to ask for advice. The doctor on call, Dr. John B. Sullivan, first asked if the two had come into contact with poisonous hydrogen sulfide gas, but there was no indication that they had. He deduced that the only other poison that could result in the effects reported by Kim was cyanide poisoning. Later blood tests confirmed Sullivan's suspicions.

At the same time that Kim was finding the link to cyanide poisoning, two off-duty firefighters deduced that the culprit might be

the Tylenol capsules. According to news accounts, Jeanna Kellerman, the mother of the first victim, heard about the Janus deaths
and contacted an Arlington Heights firefighter, Philip Cappitelli,
the son-in-law of a friend, to ask for details. Cappitelli, in turn, contacted his friend, Richard Keyworth, an Elk Grove Village firefighter,
who mentioned that Mary Kellerman had taken a Tylenol capsule
before collapsing. Noting that it was "a wild stab," Keyworth suggested that the connection might be the Tylenol. Cappitelli checked
with Arlington Heights paramedics who confirmed that the Januses
had also taken Extra-Strength Tylenol capsules. He passed on his
suspicions to Arlington Heights police, who retrieved the bottles
from both homes and found they had the same manufacturer's lot
number.

By early the next morning, the Cook County Medical Examiner's
office was testing the capsules still in the bottles. "I could smell the
cyanide as soon as I opened the containers," Michael Shaffer, the
county's chief toxicologist, told *Newsweek* magazine. Officials alerted
Johnson & Johnson, manufacturer of Tylenol, which quickly recalled
all batches of Extra-Strength Tylenol and regular Tylenol sent to the
Midwest and sent out a half-million mailgrams to doctors, hospitals,
and medical-supply companies alerting them of the potential danger.
Authorities descended on the manufacturing facilities in Pennsylvania and Texas that had produced the pills but found no evidence of
contamination or tampering. This prompted Illinois investigators to
conclude that the capsules most likely had been tampered with after
they had reached the stores.

Despite extensive efforts to alert the public about the situation—
Chicago police cruised through neighborhoods making announce-
ments on their bullhorns while church groups and the Boy Scouts
went door-to-door to warn people not to take Tylenol—the message
wasn't heard by one more victim. On October 1, thirty-five-year-old

flight attendant Paula Prince was found dead in her North Side Chicago apartment after taking a couple of Extra-Strength Tylenol.

One of the immediate results of the deaths was the introduction of improved tamper-proof packaging for over-the-counter medicines. Within months of the murders, drug manufacturers had changed the way their products were packaged to include glued boxes, plastic coverings over the bottles, foil seals, and shrink-wrapping.

Meanwhile, authorities found additional cyanide-tainted capsules in bottles that had been recalled from Chicago area stores and tested. At the time, they expressed optimism that prints might be found that would help them find the killer. By October 1982, police believed they had a break in the case. A handwritten letter was sent to Johnson & Johnson threatening more deaths if the company didn't pay $1 million. The letter instructed the company to deposit the money into a Chicago bank account that was traced to thirty-eight-year-old James W. Lewis, a tax accountant with a checkered past. Following a national manhunt, Lewis was arrested in a reading room of a New York Public Library annex in December. Ultimately, Lewis was convicted of sending the letter—which he later admitted doing. Lewis insisted he had sent the letter in an attempt to embarrass his wife's former employer—the money was to be paid into the employer's bank account—and he never intended to collect any of it. Law enforcement authorities, however, acknowledged there was nothing that linked Lewis to the poisonings and indicated he was an opportunist simply trying to take advantage of the situation.

Or was he?

When he was taken into custody, Lewis described in great detail to investigators his theory on how the killer probably committed the act. According to news accounts, he diagrammed all of the steps necessary to pull off such a crime including how to buy the medicine, the best method for inserting cyanide into the capsules, and how to return the tainted product undetected onto a store shelf. In a later interview he said he was only trying to help authorities figure out how the poison had made its way into the Tylenol capsules. "I was doing like I would have done for a corporate client, making a list of possible scenarios," Lewis told the Associated Press.

After serving twelve years for writing the extortion letter, Lewis was released from prison and relocated to the Boston area. In 2007, on the twenty-fifth anniversary of the murders, the FBI and Illinois authorities restarted the stalled investigation. In a statement, the Bureau said it was taking a fresh look at the evidence in light of more recent "advances in forensic technology." In February 2009, FBI agents, who long considered Lewis a prime suspect but couldn't prove anything, searched his condominium and a rented storage facility in Cambridge and were seen removing boxes and an Apple computer. In January 2010, the Middlesex Superior Court in Massachusetts ordered Lewis and his wife to submit DNA and fingerprint samples. Despite the new flurry of interest in Lewis and the case, however, no charges have yet been filed.

As for Lewis, he has steadfastly maintained his innocence in various media interviews and has a website on which he protests that he has been unfairly targeted. In October 2010, he told Chicago investigative reporter Chuck Goudie, "There never was a Tylenol Killer." In an e-mail sent to Goudie, Lewis insisted that Johnson & Johnson had invented the story of there being a Tylenol murderer in order to "outsource liability." He blamed the company's lax safety standards for the poisoned capsules, saying it was a corporate conspiracy that had been covered up for nearly three decades. A skeptical Goudie called Lewis's account "revisionist history."

The case remains open.

THE VALENTINE'S DAY TRAGEDY

2008

University campuses are supposed to be sanctuaries—safe places where students can learn and grow. But on the afternoon of February 14, 2008—Valentine's Day—Steve Kazmierczak, a twenty-seven-year-old University of Illinois graduate student, entered a large lecture hall on the campus of Northern Illinois University (NIU), where he had previously been enrolled, and began shooting people. Within less than six minutes, Kazmierczak fired six rounds from a sawed-off Remington 12-gauge shotgun and forty-eight rounds using a 9mm semiautomatic Glock pistol. He shot and killed five students and wounded another eighteen before placing the pistol into his mouth and pulling the trigger.

While not the worst campus killing spree in U.S. history—that dubious honor goes to a Virginia Tech gunman who killed thirty-three people in 2007—the NIU shootings were certainly the worst such event in the history of the state of Illinois.

So why did he do it? In the months following the shooting, a number of articles attempted to answer the question. Writer David

Vann, who has published a book about the shootings (*Last Day on Earth: A Portrait of the NIU School Shooter, Steve Kazmierczak*) as well as an article about Kazmierczak in *Esquire* magazine, told the NIU student newspaper, the *Northern Star*, that he didn't think Kazmierczak had a motive. "Instead of looking for motive, I think we have to try to understand who he was and how it became possible for him to do what he did," Vann said. "To understand that, I think the main narratives would be his mental health history, his sexual history, his fascination with other killers and even Hitler, his fascination with horror movies (especially the *Saw* series), his Libertarian views and love of Nietzsche, his ownership of guns, and his training from the Army to kill without any emotion or psychological effect."

Steve Kazmierczak was born in Elk Grove Village, Illinois, in 1980, and was the only son of Gail and Robert Kazmierczak. He was an average student in school with a troubled personal history. In high school, he had attempted suicide several times, and after graduating from Elk Grove High School in 1998, he spent time in psychiatric facilities. In 2001, he briefly joined the Army and completed basic training but was then released when it was discovered he had lied on his application about his mental health history. About six months later, Kazmierczak enrolled at NIU and began studying sociology with an emphasis on criminology.

At NIU, Kazmierczak was able to get his life on track. While at first many of his fellow students found him a bit weird and intense— Kazmierczak's nickname in the dorms was "Strange Steve"—he did well in his classes, and at the end of four years he was given a Dean's Award, the highest undergraduate honor, and admitted into NIU's sociology graduate program. Unfortunately, he entered the program just as the school was cutting back sociology faculty, particularly in the area of criminology, so he was unable to study what interested him. In mid-2007, he transferred to the University of Illinois at Champaign (U of I) to study social work.

It was around this time that Kazmierczak became fascinated by guns. He legally purchased a Glock .45-caliber handgun, a shotgun, and another handgun, and then began spending time practicing at a shooting range. His former girlfriend, Jessica Baty, noticed little changes in his personality, such as checking multiple times if the apartment door was locked and washing his hands nearly two dozen times per day. In his *Esquire* story, Vann wrote that Kazmierczak was "anxious and worried about everything, paranoid . . . he has these mood swings, totally out of control, and he gets really irritable, picks fights with Jessica [his girlfriend]." At her urging, he visited the campus health center and was prescribed Prozac (an antidepressant) and Xanax (an antianxiety drug), which seemed to help.

After a few months at U of I, Kazmierczak decided to become a part-time student and also work as a correctional officer at the Rockville Correctional Facility in Indiana. According to Vann, he quickly realized the job wasn't what he expected—it was less about rehabilitation and more about just moving inmates from place to place—but he enjoyed the training, particularly when he was taught how to use a Remington 12-gauge shotgun.

At the same time, Kazmierczak was clearly struggling with inner demons. He began engaging in random sexual encounters with women he met via the Internet and collected more guns and ammunition, including his own Remington 12-gauge shotgun. He went on and off his meds—the Prozac gave him acne—and had several tattoos etched on his arms, including a pentagram and the character Jigsaw from the *Saw* horror films.

On February 11, while his roommate/former girlfriend was at work, he sat in the apartment they shared and sawed off the barrel of his shotgun. He packed the shotgun into a guitar case, tossed three handguns and an assortment of loaded magazines into a duffel bag, made his bed, and drove three hours north to DeKalb, home of NIU. He checked into a run-down motel and spent the next two days talking to friends on his phone, writing e-mails, and buying gifts online, including a wedding ring, for Baty, his former girl-friend. On the evening of February 13, he erased all of his online mail and closed his e-mail accounts. He removed the SIM card from his cell phone as well as the hard drive from his laptop and hid them someplace (they have never been found).

At 3:04 p.m., Kazmierczak parked in a lot near Cole Hall on the NIU campus. On his car's CD player was Marilyn Manson's "The Last Day on Earth." According to the police report, he entered the backstage area of Cole Hall Auditorium 101, which has a seating capacity of 464 although only about 120 students were in attendance that day for Geology 104—Introduction to Ocean Sciences. He was wearing a black knit cap, dark jeans, a pair of dark brown boots, and a black T-shirt with the word "Terrorist" printed across the chest. He was carrying a black guitar case containing the shotgun and armed with three handguns and a spring-loaded knife.

"Kazmierczak walked a short distance across the stage and opened fire with the shotgun directly into the audience," noted the investigative summary prepared by NIU's Department of Public Safety. "Once the shooter had expended all immediately available rounds from the shotgun, he discarded it on the west end of the stage and began firing at the room's occupants with a 9mm Glock semi-automatic pistol. Kazmierczak is reported to have walked up and down the west aisle and directly in front of or on the stage, firing the weapon as he went."

The room was quiet by the time police entered the hall at about 3:11 p.m. The transcript of the dispatch report notes that sergeant Larry Ellington, who entered the hall near the stage, said on the radio: "Shooter's down. Shotgun's secure. We need an ambulance and the coroner at Cole Hall."

In the initial news stories, Kazmierczak was described as an "outstanding" student. NIU police chief Donald Grady told the media there were "no red flags" in Kazmierczak's background that could have predicted he would snap. Vann, however, told CNN that there were plenty of signs. "At some point after you look at all of those records, you have to wonder, what does a mass murderer have to do to get noticed?" he asked.

In the aftermath of the tragedy, there were calls by Governor Rod Blagojevich and NIU President John G. Peters to demolish Cole Hall, leave the site as a memorial, and erect a new auditorium nearby that would be called Memorial Hall. The $40 million price tag on such a project, however, made it unlikely it would ever be done. In 2009, the NIU Board of Trustees approved a more modest $9.5 million plan to completely remodel the building and convert the lecture hall where the shootings occurred into the NIU Anthropological Museum.

BLAGO'S RISE AND FALL

2009

In the beginning, Rod Blagojevich seemed like the kind of white knight who could ride into the ethically challenged wilderness of the Illinois political system and vanquish the forces of corruption. It was a strong message, particularly to an electorate that had seen three previous recent governors (Democrats Otto Kerner and Dan Walker as well as Republican George Ryan) convicted of various crimes. In his three terms in the U.S. Congress, from 1997 to 2002, Blagojevich hadn't made much of an impression, although he once helped the Reverend Jesse Jackson free three captive U.S. prisoners of war in Yugoslavia. When he ran successfully for governor in 2002, he did so as a reform candidate, an antidote to the scandal-ridden administration of outgoing governor George Ryan. In his inaugural address on January 14, 2003, the boyish-looking forty-seven-year-old governor with a mop of thick, dark hair pledged to reject "the politics of mediocrity and corruption" and said he would "govern as a reformer."

It would be the high point of his career as a reformer.

After about two years in office, Blagojevich, called "Blago" by the Chicago media, became embroiled in allegations that campaign donors were being rewarded with state jobs and appointments. "Like presidents giving ambassadorships and honorary posts to political allies, Illinois governors have long appointed friends and contributors to state positions," the *Chicago Tribune* reported on November 21, 2004. "Yet an examination of Blagojevich's appointments provides the latest example of how a governor who vowed to end business as usual in state government has appeared to perpetuate it in at least some respects. Blagojevich has made about seven hundred appointments to state boards, commissions and agencies since becoming governor in January 2003. A *Tribune* analysis of public records found that many of those appointees, their companies, groups they are affiliated with or their relatives have contributed almost $1.9 million to the governor."

After Blagojevich had a falling-out with his father-in-law, a powerful Chicago alderman named Richard Mell who had helped Blagojevich get elected to Congress and as governor, Mell publicly alleged that his son-in-law had indeed been exchanging appointments to state boards and commissions in return for campaign contributions. Mell later recanted the charges under threat of a lawsuit by the governor. By January 2005, "reform" Governor Blagojevich was being investigated by federal prosecutors for his administration's hiring practices. In perhaps the most bizarre revelation, Blagojevich was accused of giving a $45,000-per-year state position to the wife of a close friend and campaign contributor in return for a $1,500 check made out to the governor's seven-year-old daughter. "This is a very normal, typical thing that happens between close friends and families," Blagojevich said at the time. Despite the growing allegations of corruption, Blagojevich was reelected governor in November 2006.

Earlier that same year, two fund-raisers for Blagojevich, Antoin "Tony" Rezko and Stuart Levine, were indicted for soliciting kickbacks from businesses seeking to obtain state contracts. While Blagojevich was not charged in the indictments, government prosecutors identified him as the intended beneficiary of several of Rezko's extortion efforts. In 2008, after being convicted on sixteen of twenty-four counts, Rezko agreed to cooperate with prosecutors, who subsequently indicted others in Blagojevich's inner circle.

The noose tightened on the governor when, on December 9, 2008, FBI agents arrested Blagojevich and his chief of staff, John Harris, on twenty-four counts of conspiracy to commit mail fraud and wire fraud as well as for soliciting bribes. Federal prosecutors alleged that Blagojevich had attempted to sell the vacant U.S. Senate seat formerly held by President Barack Obama. In wiretap recordings released by federal authorities, the governor could be heard saying about the vacant Senate seat, "I've got this thing and it's [expletive] golden and I'm just not giving it up for [expletive] nothing."

Despite the arrest, Blagojevich resisted numerous calls for him to resign as governor. Two days after his arrest, every Democratic Party member of the U.S. Senate signed a letter demanding Blagojevich not appoint a replacement for Obama. On December 15, the Illinois House of Representatives announced it would begin impeachment proceedings to remove Blagojevich from office. Two weeks later, the governor defiantly appointed former Illinois attorney general Roland Burris to serve out the remaining two years of the Obama term. It was later revealed that Blagojevich had also considered appointing popular talk-show host Oprah Winfrey, who is based in Chicago. Although Winfrey said she was not interested, she said she thought she would make a great senator.

The Illinois Legislature moved fast on the impeachment. On January 14, the General Assembly voted 117–1 that there was sufficient cause to impeach the governor (the only vote in opposition came from his sister-in-law, state representative Deb Mell) and forwarded the charges to the Illinois State Senate. Senators conducted a brief impeachment trial on January 26–28, which Blagojevich boycotted, saying the proceedings were a nothing more than a "kangaroo court." On January 29, the Senate voted to impeach him by a unanimous vote of 59–0, making him the first governor in Illinois history to have been impeached. Just prior to the vote, Blagojevich decided to appear before the Senate to protest his innocence, saying, "How can you throw a governor out of office on a criminal complaint and you haven't been able to show or to prove any criminal activity? I'm appealing to you and your sense of fairness."

Following his impeachment, which included a ban from running for state office ever again, Blagojevich embarked on a bizarre national media campaign to defend himself and, he claimed, make money so he could pay for his legal defense. He appeared on the *Late Show with David Letterman, The Daily Show,* and *The Celebrity Apprentice* reality TV show. Additionally, his wife, Patti, appeared on *I'm a Celebrity . . . Get Me Out of Here!,* another reality show. In 2009 he released a book, *The Governor: Finally, the Truth Behind the Political Scandal That Continues to Rock the Nation,* in which he offered his side of the impeachment and his legal troubles.

On June 8, 2010, Blagojevich's trial began in Chicago with the ex-governor telling the media that the public was about to hear "all of the things I've been dying to tell you for the last year and a half." He denied he was guilty of any wrongdoing and charged federal prosecutors with having "hid the truth and . . . keeping it in a locked box." In fact, Blagojevich did not testify during the trial, nor did his attorneys call to the stand any high-profile names, such as former White House chief of staff Rahm Emanuel or U.S. senator from Illinois Dick Durbin, which had been included on the witness list.

About two months after the trial began, jurors came back with the verdict—Blagojevich was guilty of one of the twenty-four charges: lying to federal agents. The conviction carries a maximum penalty of five years in prison. Outside the courtroom, the former governor crowed about his innocence, saying that prosecutors had wasted tens of millions of taxpayer dollars. However, subsequent polling of jurors indicated that a single member of the jury had held out on at least three of the most damaging charges—conspiracy to commit extortion, attempted extortion, and conspiracy to commit bribery—allowing Blagojevich to narrowly escape being convicted of those crimes. Federal prosecutors immediately said they would retry the governor on the same charges.

So much for that white knight stuff.

SELECTED BIBLIOGRAPHY

Jolliet and Marquette Discover Illinois (1673)

Biles, Roger. *Illinois: A History of the Land and Its People*. DeKalb: Northern Illinois University Press, 2005.

Jensen, Richard. *Illinois: A History*. Champaign: University of Illinois Press, 2001.

The Americans Take Over (The Battle for Kaskaskia) (1778)

Howard, Robert P. *Illinois: A History of the Prairie State*. Grand Rapids, MI: Wm. B. Eerdmans Publishing Company, 1986.

The Black Hawk War (1832)

Jung, Patrick J. *The Blackhawk War of 1832*. Norman: University of Oklahoma Press, 2008.

The First Abolitionist Martyr: Elijah Lovejoy (1837)

Simon, Paul. *Freedom's Champion: Elijah Lovejoy*. Carbondale: Southern Illinois University Press, 1994.

The Murder of Joseph Smith (1844)

Oaks, Dallin H., and Marvin S. Hill. *Carthage Conspiracy: The Trial of the Accused Assassins of Joseph Smith*. Champaign: University of Illinois Press, 1979.

The Donner Party Tragedy: It All Began in Springfield (1846)

Stewart, George R. *Ordeal by Hunger.* Cambridge, MA: The Riverside Press, 1960.

Illinois's Great Debates (1858)

Angle, Paul M., ed. *The Complete Lincoln-Douglas Debates of 1858.* Chicago: University of Chicago Press, 1991.

Guelzo, Allen C. *Lincoln and Douglas: The Debates that Defined America.* New York: Simon & Schuster, 2009 (reprint).

The Windy City Burns (1871)

Cromie, Robert. *The Great Chicago Fire.* New York: McGraw-Hill Book Company, 1958.

Kogan, Herman, and Robert Cromie. *The Great Fire: Chicago, 1871.* New York: G. P. Putnam's Sons, 1971.

The Bizarre Plot to Ransom Abraham Lincoln's Body (1876)

Craughwell, Thomas J. *Stealing Lincoln's Body.* Cambridge, MA: The Belknap Press of Harvard University Press, 2007.

Pullman's Fight Against Free Will (1894)

Papke, David Ray. *The Pullman Case: The Clash of Labor and Capital in Industrial America.* Lawrence: University Press of Kansas, 1999.

Death Plays the Iroquois Theatre (1903)

Brandt, Nat. *Chicago Death Trap: The Iroquois Theatre Fire of 1903.* Carbondale: Southern Illinois University Press, 2003.

SELECTED BIBLIOGRAPHY

Springfield's Race Riots (1908)

Crouthamel, James L. "The Springfield Race Riot of 1908." *The Journal of Negro History* 45, no. 3 (1960).

Disaster Underground: The Cherry Mine Tragedy (1909)

Fliege, Stu. *Tales and Trails of Illinois.* Champaign: University of Illinois Press, 2002.

Stout, Steve. "Tragedy in November: The Cherry Mine Disaster." *Journal of the Illinois State Historical Society 72,* no. 1 (February 1979).

The East St. Louis Race Riot (1917)

Lumpkins, Charles L. *American Pogrom: The East St. Louis Race Riot and Black Politics.* Athens: Ohio University Press, 2008.

Rudwick, Elliott. *Race Riot at East St. Louis, July 2, 1917 (Blacks in the New World).* Champaign: University of Illinois Press, 1982.

The Herrin Massacre (1922)

Angle, Paul M. *Bloody Williamson: A Chapter in American Lawlessness.* New York: Alfred A. Knopf, 1952.

Killer Twister (1925)

Akin, Wallace E. *The Forgotten Storm: The Great Tri-State Tornado of 1925.* Guilford, CT: Lyons Press, 2004.

Felknor, Peter S. *The Tri-State Tornado.* Lincoln, NE: iUniverse Inc., 2004.

The Williamson County War (1926)

DeNeal, Gary. *A Knight of Another Sort: Prohibition Days and Charlie Birger.* 2nd ed. Carbondale: Southern Illinois University Press, 1998.

Pensoneau, Taylor. *Brothers Notorious: The Sheltons.* New Berlin, IL: Downstate Publications, 2002.

Scarface Goes to Jail (1931)

Kobler, John. *Capone: The Life and World of Al Capone.* New York: Albert A. Knopf, 1971.

Schoenberg, Robert. *Mr. Capone: The Real—and Complete—Story of Al Capone.* New York: Harper Paperbacks, 1993.

The G-Men Finally Get Their Man: The Shooting of John Dillinger (1934)

Burrough, Bryan. *Public Enemies: America's Greatest Crime Wave and the Birth of the FBI, 1933–34.* New York: Penguin Books, 2004.

Matera, Dary. *John Dillinger: The Life and Death of America's First Celebrity Criminal.* Cambridge, MA: Da Capo Press, 2005.

Tale of Two Tragedies (1947 & 1951)

Hartley, Robert E., and David Kenney. *Death Underground: The Centralia and West Frankfort Mine Disasters.* Carbondale: Southern Illinois University Press, 2006.

Chicago's Big Show Trial (1969)

Schultz, John. *The Chicago Conspiracy Trial.* New York: Da Capo Press, 1993.

The Valentine's Day Tragedy (2008)

Vann, David. *Last Day on Earth: A Portrait of the NIU Shooter, Steve Kazmierczak*. New York: HarperCollins Books, 2011.

Blago's Rise and Fall (2009)

Blagojevich, Rod. *The Governor: Finally, the Truth Behind the Political Scandal That Continues to Rock the Nation*. Beverly Phoenix Books, 2009.

INDEX

ABOUT THE AUTHOR

Richard Moreno is the author of twelve books, including *Illinois Curiosities* and three other books published by Globe Pequot. In 2007, he was honored with the Nevada Writers Hall of Fame Silver Pen Award. He currently serves as a journalism instructor and director of student publications at Western Illinois University. He resides in Macomb, Illinois.